WALK

WITH GOD

HENRY MIRANDA

Copyright © 2015

Disclaimer

All the material contained in this book is provided for educational and informational purposes only. No responsibility can be taken for any results or outcomes resulting from the use of this material.

While every attempt has been made to provide information that is both accurate and effective, the author does not assume any responsibility for the accuracy or use/misuse of this information.

Acknowledgements

My Unending appreciation goes to THE TRINITY.

My Profound thanks to Alice Miranda and Tommy Miranda Hearn, who supported me in writing this book. And Especially the Holy Spirit, for making it possible to write this book

Preface

The purpose of this book is to help develop and maintain a closer walk with God. God is always with us; even when we think that we have been abandoned by God. Because of the many difficult situations and trials we face in our lives. During those difficult situations and trials we think we are alone, but God is even more present with us to strengthen us.

There will always be false teachers who will try to steer you away from God. But don't allow them to separate you from God. We are the ones in need of God so we need to get back to that fellowship that God and Adam once had in the garden of Eve before the disobedience of Adam.

Table of Contents

FOREWORD

God never intended for us to be alone. When God created Adam He did not allow him to be alone, but created Eve, so that he could have someone to share his life with. God knew that Adam needed someone to have fellowship with because God was not always physically present with him. You must remember that all God wants is what's best for us. He is not a mean tyrant who demands too much from us.

The hope of this book is to help someone develop and maintain a closer walk with God. We need to learn to listen to God's voice and walk and act like a Christian 100% of the time. God is always with us; even when we feel as if we have been abandoned because of the trials and difficult situations in our lives.

When we were in the world, we behaved like the world. Now that we belong to God, we should act not as the world, but as a child of God. God loves us and doesn't want us to fall away from Him. He is constantly working in our lives so that we can be closer to Him. Are we pretending that we belong to God, but all the while we are our own person?

life means. In God, there is no condemnation, guilt, weakness, defeat, despair, want and no separation. Hope is always centered on the coming of the Lord. We must live in a way that is pleasing and honoring to God. Sin destroys health, relationships, finances, and the fulfillment of your purpose in life. Salvation is God's on-going rescuing and delivering power. God has provided all we need to overcome every attack of the enemy.

Satan's goal is to keep us from establishing and maintaining a relationship with God. If he fails, and we come to know God, Satan tries to keep us from growing and developing a deeper relationship with God. Satan's desire to keep us from experiencing God's love in our life—to keep us from having God's presence and power actively at work in us. God desires for His word to change us, renew our minds, change our habits, strengthen our self-control, and expand our ability to express love. It will also renew our willingness to forgive and to show mercy, and enlarge our capacity for joy, patience, and kindness.

When we are strong in our faith and filled with hope and the power and presence of the Holy Spirit, we are not going to fall victim to our enemy's attack of temptation. We will always win the battle with the power of Christ in us..

CHAPTER 1:
FELLOWSHIP WITH GOD

"The first and chief need of our Christian life is, Fellowship with God. The divine life within us comes from God, and is entirely dependent upon Him. As I need every moment afresh the air to breathe, as the sun, every moment afresh sends down its light, so it is only in direct living communication with God that my soul can be strong"

"This is the message which we have heard from Him and declare to you, that God is light and in Him is no darkness at all. If we say that we have fellowship with Him, and walk in darkness, we lie and do not practice the truth. But if we walk in the light as He is in the light, we have fellowship with one another, and the blood of Jesus Christ, His Son cleanses us from all sin." **- 1 John 1:5-7 (NKJV)**

In the beginning, God created man to have fellowship with Him. When God created Adam he did not let him be alone, he created Eve, and so he could have someone to share his life with. God knew that Adam needed someone to have fellowship with him, because God was not always physically present with him most of the time. Mankind instead, chose to go his own way when he disobeyed God's instruction in the Garden of Eden, and fellowship with God was broken. This self-will, exhibited today by an attitude of active rejection or passive indifference, is an evidence of what God's word calls sin.

Before the fall, Adam and Eve had uninterrupted fellowship with God, but after they sinned the relationship was vastly changed. Instead of going out to meet God, they hid themselves from the presence of the Lord. What a sad change. Before they sinned, if they heard the voice of God coming, they probably ran to meet him with a humble joy welcoming his gracious visits. But now God had become a terror to them. They hid themselves from God because their intimate fellowship with God was broken. Sin breaks our fellowship with God, and when fellowship with Him is broken, peace is broken.

Since GOD is holy and man is sinful, there is a great divide, which separates us. Some of us continually try to reach God through our own efforts, such as leading a 'good' life, acting ethically, having high morals, using deep philosophy, etc. But we fail miserably. Being without God's fellowship leads to loneliness and isolation, God gave us a way that we may have fellowship with him. It is through his only Son. It is only through salvation that we can have fellowship with God. *John 3:16*. Having God's fellowship means we can always have someone to help guide us in our direction in life. We don't have to make decisions on our own; we have someone we can talk to and ask advice in making the right decisions. God created us to fellowship with him. Lacking that fellowship, we may find ourselves miserable and disoriented at times.

Most of us go through our daily lives without even thinking of having fellowship with our Creator. Why are we lonely at times, even when we are with friends? Is it because we were never intended to be alone in the first place? That emptiness remains, even when we think we are financially secure and happy. We may not know why we feel so empty and lonely, so we struggle alone not knowing how to rid ourselves of the loneliness. But it is the fellowship of God that we are missing

Most of our problems come from feeling alone. So it drives us to things that we think would remove the loneliness. Some of us become workaholics, some turn to drinking, or medication (drugs) to take away that lonely feeling. We are human beings, and we have been given a mind to be able to reason thinks out with, but we can't talk to ourselves. We need to discuss things with other people. We need fellowship, and if we don't have it, we may get lonely and depressed at times.

It's a hard thing being without anyone to talk with. We may think we are self-sufficient and don't need anyone, but that is where we are wrong. We were made to have fellowship, and we will always feel alone until we get back to the fellowship God intended us to have with Him from the beginning of time when he created us. The main reason we are without fellowship is because we are too busy trying to get ahead in life. We forget all about God and want to do things our way.

We were not put on this earth without a purpose. We cannot be aimless workers striving all the time with no end reward. Our purpose in life is to have fellowship with our Creator. God did not want people that were servers only, but the ones who would voice their own opinion. How can you have a conversation with someone who does not have an opinion? When you get together with friends, everyone voices, their own ideas because no one thinks the same. So it is with God.

He created the human race to have someone to talk to as a father would talk and instruct his son. God gave us a freewill. Freewill is being able to make your own decisions, not like a puppet that can only do as his master pulls the strings. Our goal should always be to have deep fellowship with God. Our hearts were purified at salvation, and we began to live in the presence of God. We began to see and to comprehend him more fully when our spiritual eyes were opened. And because of our freewill, we can choose to be a follower of Christ or follow the ways of the world.

As Christians, we must have fellowship with one another in order to stay strong in the faith. One of the main reasons we go to church is to have fellowship with others in Christ, so we can stay strong in the Lord. You may remember that old saying. "Tell me your friend, and I will tell you who you are." The company we keep is very important for our spiritual growth. If we hang around bad company because we think we are strong enough to resist temptation we are wrong and only fooling our self's. Don't put yourself in harm's way.

We need to have fellowship with other Christians so we can mature in the Lord. We need to be around Christians for strength and moral support to help us from falling back. We must realize what wonderful blessings can come out of a good Christian fellowship. The manna of one day was corrupt when the next day came. It is very important that we have fresh grace from heaven everyday, and this can only be obtained by direct waiting upon God Himself. Begin each day by tarrying before God, and letting Him touch you. Take time to hear him.

*Not forsaking the assembling of ourselves together, as is the manner of some, but exhorting one another, and so much the more as you see the Day approaching- **Hebrews 10:25 (NKJV)***

In the same way that we spend time with God in order to grow, we need to spend time with other Christians. To become encouraged in our faith and realize that we're not alone when we are facing struggles or experiencing joy. Our fellowship with one another to see where we need to grow and what behavior or ideas we have that might be damaging to our faith.

We need friends, and Christian friends are more likely to identify with the spiritual struggles and joys we experience. As Christians, we can easily open the door to doing things we shouldn't do, or entertaining ideas that can hurt us spiritually. But Christian friends will warn us when they see these things, but if we don't have these friends, how would you know that you are going off your path.

Fellowship" is the evidence of walking in the light

*If we say that we have fellowship with Him, and walk in darkness, we lie and do not practice the truth. But if we walk in the light as He is in the light, we have fellowship with one another, and the blood of Jesus Christ, His Son cleanses us from all sin-1 **John 1:6-7** (NKJV)*

By fellowshipping with other Christians, it makes us stronger and better in our faith. If we are not careful, many things in life can turn you away from God. We need fellowship with other Christians to keep us strong in God. Christian fellowship is critical! Being in the company of people who think like you do is very important. Christian fellowship is essential for your spiritual growth and survival as a Christian.

As you meditate on this wondrous salvation and seek full fellowship with the great and HOLY God, wait on Him to reveal Christ in you, and you will feel how important to giving up everything and receive Him. Seek the grace to know what it means to live as wholly for God as Christ did. Only the Holy Spirit Himself can teach yielding entirely the whole life to God mean. If you wait on God and fellowship with Him, He will definitely show you what you do not know. Let every approach to God, and every request for fellowship with Him be accompanied by a new, very definite and entire surrender to Him to work in you.

CHAPTER 2:
CREATED EQUAL

Have you ever felt you were treated less than equal because of not having the proper upbringing up, schooling, appearance, or speech? Society has a way of separating us into different groups. To be accepted in today's society, you have to have all the right credentials. I was born in South Texas. I remember going into a department store when I was young where there were two drinking fountains, one marked for whites only and the other marked for colored only. The restrooms were the same way. I didn't understand it at that time. Like everybody else, I just lived with it. I never met a black person until the age of eleven and we lived in different parts of town.

I remember one particular incident to this day. I was walking with some friends in downtown Houston. We were walking on the sidewalk when this black person came around the corner. We were about ready to move out of the way, when he stepped off the sidewalk and into the street to avoid us. I learned later that he was considered a lower class citizen and he was expected to make a way for us.

In 1955, I received an invitation from my older brother to visit him in California. He had lived in California since his discharge from the Air Force after serving in Korea. My brother sent me a bus ticket so I could travel from Houston, Texas to Los Angeles, California. As the bus made its way to California, it made several stops.

In Arizona I was surprised to see that a black person got on board, and instead of going to the back of the bus, which is what I was accustomed to, he sat next to me. I didn't know how to act. I had never been close to a black man before. He broke the ice and started to tell me he was going home, and that he was from Oakland, California. I got to know him, and that changed my whole outlook on black people. I know now what is meant by the old expression "*walk a mile in my shoes and you will know me*" I really enjoyed his company and our conversation made the long trip easier to bear.

We are all created equal in the eyes of God. He doesn't see any color or achievements that would get us closer to Him. Jesus paid the price for us to be all one family with God our Father. We all start at the same place when we enter the Kingdom of God. The high privilege of the children of God is that we are created equally. Here is one of the thing describing the privilege; "*We are ever with God*". For example in the Old Testament times. We are told that " *Enoch walked with God* ". We should realize that every children of God is called to this blessed privilege, to live every moment of his or her life in fellowship with God. We are called to enjoy the full light of His countenance.

Most everybody has heard about or even played the game Monopoly. In the start of the game each player is given the same amount of money. The object of the game is to buy as much property as possible with the money given and to bankrupt your opponent by requiring them to pay rent when they land on your properties. You get rich quick, especially if you have houses and hotels on them. It's the same when we start out in life. In the movie Forrest Gump, he makes a statement "*life is like a box of candy you never know what you are going to get*" Basically, that is "*life is what you make of it*". We can excel in education and go forward, or we can just let life go by mindlessly.

Jesus used parables to teach his listeners about the Kingdom of God. What is a parable? *A parable is a story that conveys a moral truth*. Parables tell a story, not about something recurrent in real life, but about a one-time event which is fictitious. They derive their persuasiveness from being told in a simple, vivid, and fresh way which engages the hearer.

In the parable of the worker in the vineyard for example, this parable basically means there is no seniority with God and that we are all equal. (Matthew 20: 1-16) The master of the field hired some day laborers in the morning and set the amount of pay. In the middle of the afternoon he went out and hired new labors and offered to pay them the same as the ones who were hired earlier. In the latter part of the afternoon, he went out to hire some more laborers to work in his field. That evening he paid off his workers and he paid them all the same. The morning's laborers were upset because the late workers received the same amount of money as they did.

The laborers who worked all day complained to the master because he paid the afternoon laborers the same wage. And they had worked all day. It doesn't matter at what age we became Christians, we are all going to be rewarded equally according to our faithfulness.

Many Christians have the attitude

"People in my church should do things my way

because I've been here longer." No person should feel *"there's no point in becoming a Christian now. I have lived such a terrible life that even if I became a Christian, I would get little or no reward."*

God does not care how long you did not follow Him. His care is when your life on earth ends, were you a follower of Christ or not? God loves His people too much to withhold His fellowship from them for any such reason. We should know that the true reason of the absence of God from us is rather to be found in our sin and unbelief, than in any supposed sovereignty of His. If the child of God is walking in faith and obedience, the Divine presence will be enjoyed in unbroken continuity.

We are all in the same position in Christ. We made the choice to follow Christ because God allows us the freedom to choose. We were not forced to serve God, so why do we act as if we are? God is our master because we chose to be slaves to him. The position we hold in the church should not matter; the only thing we should be worried about is; are we serving God to the best of our potential. If you were 10 years old or 80 years old when you accepted Christ as your Savior, you are only at the beginning, because you were reborn in the spirit, you received a new birth.

Give no thought of what time you have left in your lives to serve Christ. Only God knows that. Just do what God has for you to do. The reward is eternal life with our Master. Take the ants, for example. They live in a colony and each has a single purpose in life and that is to serve the colony. They have worker ants and army ants and ants that serve the queen. They do not look at their co-workers to see who is working harder or who is working slowly, they just perform their duty to the best of their ability.

No matter what position we hold, it leads to the same reward: eternal life with God. We are not like the ants who do not have a free will to make decisions. Remember that we are all equal in the eyes of God, and do not concern yourself with what others are doing or not doing. Just continue to serve God in the area He has selected for you.

CHAPTER 3:
SIN: OUR OWN DEMISE

For all have sinned and fall short of the glory of God-**Romans 3:23 (NKJV)**

God placed Adam and Eve in the Garden of Eden and forbid them to eat fruit from the "tree of knowledge" good and evil. Everything was good until Satan the fallen angel entered into the picture. Consider God's statement here: "You are free to eat from any tree in the garden; but you must not eat from the tree of the knowledge of good and evil, for when you eat of it you will surely die." (Genesis 2:16-17)

The Scriptures say: "When the woman saw that the fruit of the tree was good for food and pleasing to the eye, and also desirable for gaining wisdom, she took some and ate it. She also gave some to her husband, who was with her, and he ate it." (Gen. 3:6) After they sinned in Genesis 3, God sentenced them to die as per Genesis 2:17 (Genesis 3:19), and that was in part why they were forbidden to take from the Tree of Life: had they eaten that fruit of the tree of life they would have lived forever.

Because of their rebellion, they were removed from the Garden of Eden and the world fell into a fallen state, and suffered the degrading and deadly consequences of sinfulness. Now, because of the fall of man, and because of this act of disobedience all mankind has a sinful nature. Romans 5:12 (NKJV) Therefore, through one man sin entered the world and death through sin. And thus, death spread to all men because all have sinned.

We all possess a sinful nature that we inherited from Adam. Whether we like it or not, that is the way it is! We are all born sinners and must die because we come from Adam. The first man who disobeyed God's commandment is our forefather and we are just like him. Who among us can say he has never disobeyed the commandments of God? Not a single one of us! Like a horrible contagious disease, the sin that was in Adam has spread to us all Just as an epidemic is not confined to the one from whom it originates.

What exactly is sin anyway? The truth is that sin, as defined in the original translations of the Bible, means "to miss the mark." The mark, in this case, is the standard of perfection established by God and evidenced by Jesus. Viewed in that light, it is clear that we are all sinners. The good news in all of this is that once we recognize ourselves as sinners, we need only to repent and embrace Jesus to be forgiven. Jesus can forgive us because He died and rose again three days later in victory over sin and death.

Sin caused man's separation from God. However, God loves us so much that He provides for us the way back into good fellowship with Him through Jesus Christ. His steadfast lovingkindness leads us back to repentance, and His grace and mercy forgives us of all our sins even though none of us deserves this forgiveness. No one can earn forgiveness and reconciliation with God. It is a free gift to those who believe and accept it by faith. Sin is an offense or rebellion against God.

Sin is what separates us from God. Remember that to stay in a state of rebellion is death. The devil stays busy at work keeping us in sin and away from God. Yet, those who continue to live in this state of rebellion against God have not lost their opportunity to be God's child. All they need do is repent. We don't have to sin. We sin by choice. You must want to serve God with all your heart, body, and soul to stay away from sin.

A desire to sin is simply a way of expressing your disbelief that God's way is best. God gave us free will and we must decide on our own how we want to lead our life. The world's way was easy, and we fell into its trap.

The world is good at presenting a great illusion (false perception) of itself so that it can look enticing. God gave us the choice to serve Him or the prince of this world, the devil. There is no excuse for sin. Man has always had the opportunity to know God and do His will according to the light of nature and conscience.

From the very first sin, it has been a matter of willfulness. No one can say, "I could not help it." Remember that "No temptation has overtaken you except what is common to mankind. And God is faithful; he will not let you be tempted beyond what you can bear. But when you are tempted, he will also provide a way out so that you can endure it." 1 Corinthians 10:13

> **Unforgiveness** is one way the devil always takes advantage of anyone who refuses to forgive someone. Holding unforgiveness makes us vulnerable to his attacks. The devil uses the unforgiveness that we have for others in our life to claim his right to work in our lives.

It is very important to know that we cannot receive forgiveness from God unless we practice it toward others. When we hold unforgiveness in our heart, it puts us in a prison of guilt, unable to receive our own needed forgiveness from God.

Living under guilt will hinder us in times of trials. Unforgiveness is a spirit, an evil spirit. Some of us may be engulfed in unforgiveness. Unforgiveness may cause bitterness, resentment, hatred, violence, temper, anger, retaliation, distrust, envy, suspicion, jealousy, and rebellion.

You must never permit any unforgiveness to enter your mind. No matter what someone has done or said about you, you must not allow it to affect your daily walk with Jesus.

Remember, you are the light of the world, and everyone is watching. You must let your light shine that people may see your good works of forgiveness at your job, home, school, church, and even when driving your car.

> ➢ **Rebellion** is another tool of the devil. The devil rebelled against God. And he tries real hard to get us to also rebel against God.

Rebellion is to know to do right, but have a wrong attitude so we go on strike against God refusing to do anything that pleases Him. Obstinate and stubborn sin produce a life following the wrong path. Pride is rebellion against God because it attributes to self the honor and glory due to God. Rebellion against God keeps us from experiencing the highest possible good.

We must always guard against being rebellious. There are many Christians who have fallen away from Christ and are ashamed to come back because of the sins they committed. We all sin at times, sometimes without knowing it. That is why Jesus said to pray and ask for forgiveness every day. Jesus delivered us from our trespasses and sins.

Who are we to condemn others for falling into sin from time to time? The Bible says that all have sinned and came short of the glory of God. Everybody sins at one time or another, because we are not immune to sin. With God's grace, all we have to do is ask for forgiveness, and we are as white as snow again.

Sin is missing the divine mark or coming short of the glory of God, which is his selfless love (agape love). We are born slaves to sin, and no matter how hard we try we fall short of the mark.

That is why the Gospel is our only hope of salvation. We have a free will to choose between accepting Christ's righteousness offered in the Gospel and rejecting it. We have to choose between sin and genuine righteousness.

God is both Holy and infinite. Therefore, he is infinitely holy. Consequently, even the smallest sin is infinitely offensive to him. The Bible teaches that even the smallest sin is enough to eternally separate man from God. God cannot allow sin in his presence.

We can thank God he has given us an advocate to stand up for us, his son Jesus. The devil will use our sins against us to make us feel unworthy to be a follower of Christ. The devil is a liar; don't fall into his traps or snares. He will say whatever it takes to keep us from being a follower of Christ. Don't fall prey to any of his scams.

However, when we ask for forgiveness, Jesus removes sin from our lives, forever. The devil remembers the sin, but Jesus said, "all your sins are forgiven: past, present, and future." He will never bring them up again.

A thing to remember: Don't let the guilt of your sin keep you away from Jesus. All we have to do is ask for forgiveness, and the sin will be blotted out. Guilt is only one of the many tools Satan uses against us to make us feel unworthy to serve Christ.

Author's Note:

A very important fact to remember; just because we can ask for forgiveness daily; it does not give us a license to sin.

There is no such thing as a small sin. Sin is sin. The color black is black. If you try to make it less black by adding white, it will not make a difference, because it will still be black, not gray. You have to remove the black completely, then you have no sin.

How can we call ourselves Christian if we find the things of God hard to follow, but the things the world has to offer so easy? A desire to sin is simply a way of expressing our disbelief that God's way is best.

How can we fight ourselves? Because that is exactly what we must do to stay away from sin. We have to fight against our old nature. We must put down the will of the flesh and let the Spirit have its way. That is what we must do to stay in the spirit.

The desire to do the things that the Spirit asks and the desire of our flesh seem to be at war with each other constantly. It is common to feel that we are being pulled between a life of sin and a life of righteousness.

The old nature still wants us to do the things of the flesh. The flesh wars against the spirit and the spirit against the flesh. To overcome the flesh, we must be filled with the spirit. We can be born-again Christians, but our old nature still calls us to return to our old self (habits, attitudes, desires, and old sins). We do not have to sin. Sins are what separate us from God, yet we still sin because we want to.

We yield to the flesh because it makes us feel good, but it only lasts for a short time, until the guilt of the sin sets in. The guilt of the sin is what keeps us away from Christ. We seem to be under sin's power with no control. But, we must remember we have control through Christ who gives us the strength to overcome all the wiles of the devil.

We have victory with Christ. We can and will win over sin with the power of Jesus. We can do all things through Christ who strengthens us. He will purify us unto himself and give us rest from sin. His death has procured this, and his Word has promised this.

Many of us hate the sin we keep committing, but sometimes it's a habit we cannot get rid of. We would like to be set free even to the point of seeking help from clinics. Although our sins give pleasure for a short time, we know they are wrong. Those sins are now ruling and destroying our lives, yet we keep on sinning. Why is that?

Do we find the things of the world more pleasing than being with God? What is it that makes us want to sin? We can blame it on many things: our childhood, friends, parents, peer pressure, and maybe not knowing any better way of life. Although a lot of us have gone through some traumas that have left deep scars on our souls, many of us cannot seem to understand what makes us feel lonely and depressed at times.

We figure the only way to ease the pain is to find pleasure to fill the hurts and voids in our lives. This only leads us to sin and away from our Lord and savior Jesus Christ. We do not have to feel alone. Remember with every problem that comes along, we don't have to conquer it on our own. All we have to do is turn it over to Jesus. God has given us the strength and guidance we need to resist temptation.

Remember, we have all of God's arsenals at our disposal. God is not the author of sin. A person must accept responsibility for personal, sinful acts. We cannot evade responsibility by saying, "God made me that way" or "I cannot help myself." Similarly, we cannot blame our sin problem on Satan. Satan tempts us to do evil, but we make the choice to sin and must accept the responsibility for our evil choices. Physical, emotional, and psychological desires lead to sinful acts.

There is no invisible force that makes us sin against our will. Sin is a consciously chosen path, not an outwardly determined reflex. We sin because we choose to do so. Sin's long melancholy reign over humankind began with the very first humans.

The Bible offers no philosophical explanation for the origin of sin. Instead, the Bible narrates the story of the sin of earth's first inhabitants. It presents a world in which sin is possible and temptation is present.

The fateful choice of Eve combined with Adams willingness to share in her choice is as close as it comes to explaining the origin of sin. This account shows sin to be individual in nature. Each individual must bear responsibility for choosing to sin.

Say to God, "I have sinned and I ask for your forgiveness." Remember, sin is a forfeiture of the glories and joys of heaven. If you died tonight and stood before God, and he asked, "Why should I let you into my heaven?" What would you say? If you died right now, do you know with absolute certainty that you would go to heaven?

Sin is like a weed; no matter how many times you get rid of it, it wants to come back. It may be a continuous fight with the world system, but we must always stay on the path that leads to righteousness.

For the wages of sin is death, but the gift of God is eternal life in Christ Jesus our Lord. -**Romans 6:23 NK**

CHAPTER 4:
THE PATH

Trust in the Lord with all your heart, and lean not on your own understanding; in all your ways acknowledge Him, And He shall direct your paths - **Proverbs 3:5-6 (NKJV)**

We have two paths we can travel while we are in this world, God's path which leads to eternal life or Satan's path which leads to destruction. We have been born with a free will to choose the right path if we should walk with God, we must comply with his will and not ours. We must follow the leading of the Holy Spirit. The straight path is the one that leads to our destination.

The path of the wicked is crooked, this approach to life contrasts with the straight path of righteousness. A crooked path which is the way of the world is filled with twists and turns that if we are not careful can cause us to become stagnant in our Christian walk. If that should happen, God is there to help us to get back to the straight path.

When we were young we had no cares or responsibilities, and all the decisions were made for us, because our parents were responsible for proving us with food and shelter. It is not until we reached the age of accountability that we start to make decisions for ourselves.

Since we all have different minds, some of us matured sooner than others, so we are all at different ages when we get to the age of accountability, but everyone comes to the crossroads in life and must choose for him or herself which road he or she will take in life.

"Enter by the narrow gate; for wide is the gate and broad is the way that leads to destruction and there are many who goes by it. Because narrow is the gate and difficult is the way which leads to life, and there are few who find it- **Mathew 7: 13-14 (NKJV)**

We have been born with a free will to choose the right path. If we choose to walk with God that means we must comply with his will not ours. We must follow the leading of the Holy Spirit.

Most of us have been on hiking trails (A **trail** is usually a **path**, track or unpaved lane or road) at one time or another. When we go hiking, you always see paths which have been marked for the different directions that you can take. Someone had been there before and mark the paths to make it easy for the ones following after. The path is marked for you so you won't get lost.

I think most of us wonder how much easier our life would be if God was to mark the path that we should take in life. But God does Mark the path for us and he wrote the directions in the Bible. That is God's roadmap for all of us to follow. God knows exactly where He wants to take us. He knows the minute details of our life. He has the blueprint for our whole life already we do not have to ask Him to make a new plan for our lives all we have to do is just fit into his plan for our lives.

When we were in the world we walked the path of the world which is everything that draws you away from God. When we turn our life around to follow Jesus, we start on a different path. The path that we travel on as Christians may be difficult and hard at times because the Christian path is beset with a lot of difficulties. "because we face a lot of trials, hardships, suffering, persecution, and tribulations"

But Jesus promised us that we would never be alone. He said, "*Surely, I am with you always, even to the end of the age*".

Blinders are put on horses so they can just look straight ahead and not side to side this way they're not distracted from either side. As Christians, we need to keep our eyes looking forward on the path that God has directed us. If you look for any other guidance, then Jesus, then you have left the path which God has set up for you.

I will instruct you and teach you in the way you should go; I will guide you with M0y eye- **Psalms 32:8 (NKJV)**

So if you want God to help you with difficult decisions in your life, then seek God's will for every area of your life. If you love God with your whole heart and trust fully in him, he will direct you he wants to use your gifts and experiences to accomplish his perfect plan for your life.

Do not enter the path of the wicked, and do not walk in the way of evil- **Proverbs 4:14 (NKJV)**

*Teach me your way, O Lord, and lead me in a smooth path, because of my enemies-***Psalms 27:11 (NKJV)**

Courage will be needed to accomplish what God has for us. Especially, if our family and friends turn away, because of our Christian walk. Those who adhere to the ways of God, though they may have problems along the way, in the end they will have Eternal life.

The world calls out and tries to entice you into believing it has whatever you need to fulfill your lifestyle. But, don't fall into its trap. Keep your eyes focused on our Lord. The world is not our friend. It tries to mislead us from our righteous path. The world wants to paint an illusion to make you think it can satisfy your every need. Just remember Jesus is the only savior.

The life of victory is not in what we can do, but in what we permit God to do through us. It means an end to the self-life and an entering into the Christ-life. This will give us great confidence for our future days when we face human impossibilities. Just remember, we have God's promise that he will never leave us and he will direct our steps. God will show us how to rise and get back onto the right path should we fall off at any time. Although we may suffer the Lord's rebuke and some of the inevitable consequences of our sin, later we often see where God has used it for blessing.

We must acknowledge God in all our ways, and stay on our path no matter what comes along. The devil may put rocks (fewer problems), boulders (medium problems), or mountains (big problems) in our path to keep us from continuing, but don't let that stop us from completing our journey. For there are many out there taking other paths, choosing other goals, and trying to get you to go along. The way of God is a straight one; it is not a road that winds or shifts away from one purpose to another.

We were born in this world, but that does not mean we belong to it. *"Things of the world will pass away, only the word of God will stand forever"* This world is in darkness because it does not see or does not want to see God as the creator. When we were in the world, we stumbled along in the dark because we did not have the light to see, and we could not see the path that leads to eternal life. Those in the world are the children of darkness. We were children of darkness until we came into the light. We were transformed from darkness to light and from the power of Satan unto God. The saints are the children of light; the wicked are the children of darkness. There is no such thing as a gray area. You are either light (white) or darkness (black); it's as simple as black and white. *"I know my sheep and my sheeps know me"*

Have you ever been somewhere, where you turn on the lights and you see, what seem to be hundreds of cockroaches scurry, trying to hide? They do things in the dark where they can't be seen. That is what it was like when we were in the world. We liked the darkness because we could do anything we wanted in secret. No wonder why it is said that *"We do evil in the dark"* When God's light shined on us, we ran for cover, because we could not stand to have our evil deeds exposed. We were blinded by sin, but when we came to Christ our eyes were opened wide to God's truth. We should love the light and hate darkness.

"Do not love the world or the things in the world. If anyone loves the world, the love of the Father is not in him." -1 JOHN 2:15

Knowing that our eyes have been opened to the truth, and we are the sons of Christ, we should have no fellowship with the fruitless deeds of darkness. We are aware of the principalities, powers and the rulers of the darkness of the world. We must be strong in the Lord and the power of his might. God's Holy Spirit begins the work in our hearts; the light comes in our giving ourselves to Christ, and we are no longer in darkness. In Christ, we are new creatures, our talents and time is for Christ because all things have become new.

Once we came into the light, the mysteries of God's kingdom were revealed to us. We are the children of the light. Our light should reflect the light of God. Now that we belong to God, we should act Godly. It's a daily struggle to keep from sin, but we have the Comforter to help us. It's not as if we have to face the world on our own; we have a whole army of God's people behind us. Remember, in your hour of need, you are never alone. God said that he would never leave his beloved in the hands of the enemies.

The Holy Spirit teaches by sanctification. He opens blind eyes, gives new understanding, shines into our hearts to give us the knowledge of the glory of God in the face of Jesus Christ, and enables us to receive spiritual things in a spiritual light.

But we have the mind of Christ. The power of the Holy Spirit will uphold us through our Christian path.

As Christians, we are to conduct ourselves as Christ would (with love and compassion for others) as if he were still on this earth. People have to see the light in us without us saying anything. We have to be an example of God's good works. God demands our faith and obedience to his Word as an expression of our faith. Obedience is the way of blessing and enjoyment of all God has to offer. Disobedience brings us to darkness and despair.

We chose our path to follow. That is, we gave ourselves over to Christ. We must remember that God is the Creator, and we are the created. We decided to follow Jesus and that is what we must do with all of our body and soul. The problem isn't in starting our Christian walk, but in being able to stay on the path long enough to be able to get to our celestial home.

"It is not all those that begin the christian race shall be safe, but those who endure to the end shall be safe."

We will, at times, stumble off the path. However, we need to get back on as quickly as possible. God will always be waiting for you to get back on the path should you wander away.

Our adversary (Satan) does not want us on the path to righteousness, but he wants to see us fail. From the time we start on the path to the end, he will always oppose us. We must concentrate on staying on the right path.

Remember that sin is what prevents us from staying on the path; we get easily distracted with the things of this world.

Our old nature has been buried with Christ. We have a new life in Christ, being raised with him. In our old life, we were controlled by the values of the world. Now we are to be controlled by Christ. Non-Christians are controlled by worldly values, but we as Christians are to be controlled by the values of Christ.

When we decide to go on a trip, we make all the necessary arrangements that will make the trip enjoyable. We leave nothing to chance. We do not want anything to go wrong. So it is when we start on our path to eternal life, we must make the right preparations. The Bible says we must put on the full armor of God so we can be well protected on our path.

We must be prepared for any tricks of our enemy (Satan). He will attack us constantly with the flaming arrows of disaster, depression, distress, or loneliness. We don't want to wait until the enemy attacks and then try to get ready for the battle. We must be ready at all times and armed with God's weapons. We are to be prepared, knowing full well the enemy is just waiting for the right minute to attack our faith. He is always waiting for us to make a mistake. Be constantly on the alert for any of the arsenals that the devil may send our way.

"Be filled with the Spirit."—Ephesians, 5:18.

Sometimes it may feel we are alone on our quest and no one else is on the path with us. Just remember you are never alone. The Holy Spirit dwells in us, and we can always call our Heavenly Father to help us. Give thanks to our savior who died for us so we can have the privilege to call our Father in heaven in our hour of need.

We are a part of a great army of the Lord. We have fellow Christian brothers and sisters that will help reinforce our desire to continue on our path when we feel like we cannot go on. We never have to be alone in our daily struggles.

We chose the path to follow God, and it is up to us as Christians to walk in the light and be the light to the lost. It may be hard at times to follow Christ, but remember what James said: *"My brethren, count it all joy when ye fall into divers temptations; Knowing this, that the trying of your faith worketh patience".—James 1:2 – 3*

Gold is a precious metal and pretty, but when gold is found, it is mixed with impurities. It is not until it goes through a purifying process that it becomes a precious metal and beautiful. It has to be heated to a very high temperature to melt the ore that holds the gold. Once the ore is melted all the impurities flow to the top where they are removed, leaving the pure gold behind. So it is with us Christians. We must be purified by fire (trials). That is why James said to count it all joy when we go through trials, knowing that we are being made stronger in Christ.

We do not ever want to get too comfortable with God's blessings, especially when we become financially secure. We shouldn't think we do not need God anymore and turn away from him. Don't stop serving God when all your needs are met. All things are for God's purpose and not ours. He might want you financially secure so he can use you in some ministry. We don't know God's master plan. We must remain faithful in good times and bad.

There was a Christian man who attended church regularly with his family. He was like most of us, struggling to make ends meet. His prayer was to have his own business. God opened the door for him: an opportunity to start a small mechanic's shop. He struggled, but kept coming to church and asking for God's blessing. He started to get a lot of business, but instead of attending church regularly like he had, he started to work on Sunday to get more done. He soon became financially secure and stopped attending church altogether.

Remember, we belong to God, and he will bless us when we are in fellowship with him. Do not let yourself get to a point where you forget God's blessing and turn away from him. Stay on the path and follow God's direction, and you will never go wrong.

When you were in the world you were in darkness, but now you are of the light. God has shined a light to guide you on your pathway. Once you start your walk towards God you don't want to look back. Jesus said ***"No one who puts a hand to the plow and looks back is fit for service in the kingdom of God."*** As Christians, we must be pressing on to our final goal and we cannot deviate from the path that God has set before us.

You might wonder as to what is your direction or understanding of your path, that's where the Holy Spirit comes in, He is your guide. Sometimes we hear a lot about spiritual guides, but you have to be careful because there are demonic guides that will take you away from God. That is why it is so important to always read the Scriptures and be in constant prayer so you will not be led off your path.

We have the comforter the Holy Spirit to guide us, for he is our teacher, director and counselor to help us stay on the right path towards God. That we shall not be left to wander, self-directed, in the paths of sin into which our feet have strayed, but that the Spirit of God shall dwell within us, breaking our bondage and leading us into that other pathway of good works, which God has prepared that we should walk in.

One is not led when he goes his own way. It is only when an influence distinct from himself determines our movements that we can properly say we are led. When Paul, therefore, declares that the sons of God are *"led by the Spirit of God,"* he emphasizes, first of all, the distinction between the leading Spirit and the led sons of God. As much as this he declares with great emphasis – *that there is a power within us, not ourselves, that makes for righteousness*. And he identifies this extraneous power by the Spirit of God.

The Holy Spirit, is a power dwelling in our bodies and that power that dwells in us gives motives and strength and everything needed to stay on the path that God has set before us. The Holy Spirit is an active agent in our progress towards God. We can enjoy the gracious ministry of the Holy Spirit as we believe God's word and yield to the Holy Spirit. We do things through the power of the Holy Spirit rather than through our own abilities.

"We can do all things through Christ that strengthening us."

There's only one path that can lead to heaven. And just because it seems difficult at times, it doesn't mean you will not make it. Because all you have to do is lean on Jesus and he will carry you most of the way. For we are fragile people, we are weak on our own, but through Jesus, we are strong because he gives us the strength to overcome all obstacles that come against us.

The Holy Spirit is God's guidance for our lives. God's guidance implies that we live according to the path which he has laid down for us so that our lives have a purpose in the present as well as a destiny for the future. Because we have a destiny we become pilgrims. The New Testament explicitly tells us that we are pilgrims 1 Peter 1:1.

As Christian we have a purpose and a destiny. And that is to follow the path that God has laid out for us. The Holy Spirit is to guide our lives so that it may reflect the glory of his son. We must walk worthy, adopting a lifestyle which is truly in the will of God. We are not to live in doubt and uncertainty. Jesus does not, after giving us general directions, leave us to guess the way. He leads us in a straight path.

People are too willing to believe their teachers without careful thought and prayerful investigation of God's word. One of the last promises which the Savior gave to His disciples was, may the Lord strengthen you with all might, according to His glorious power—"that you may live a life worthy of the Lord and may please Him in every way—bearing fruit in every good work, growing in the knowledge of God!"

© A CLOSER WALK WITH GOD 52

CHAPTER 5:
SPIRITUAL WARFARE

For though we walk in the flesh, we do not war according to the flesh.

For the weapons of our warfare are not carnal but mighty in God for pulling down strongholds,

*Casting down arguments and every high thing that exalts itself against the knowledge of God, bringing every thought into captivity to the obedience of Christ-***2 Corinthians 10:3-5 (NKJV)**

Have you ever walked down a dark street by yourself? If you ever have at one time or another, you might have had the feeling that someone was following you, or that someone may be trying to rob you. It's scary walking late at night alone. Nobody likes the feeling of being alone and scared.

Fear can be an awful thing. We all have fear of something and that's because we live in this world that belong to Satan. Living in this world is like constantly being in darkness and never knowing what you are up against and in constant fear always. Remember that we don't have to fear anything because we don't belong to this world of Satan.

Our world is light and we have a path that is lit for us so we can see everything. Satan wants to keep you in fear and away from God. Remember that a soul under Satan's power and led captive by him is blind to the things of God.

Author's Note:

Just remember this; if Satan is attacking you, you are on the right path with God. Satan only leaves you alone when you belong to him.

I remember when I first became a Christian; I would have the scariest dreams. One dream that comes to mind is about some wild wolves that were chasing me in a graveyard. They had backed me up against a gravestone and I started to kick them. I kept kicking them in my dream, but in reality I was kicking my wife. I had never been so frightened in my life.

Satan tries to use fear. Just remember this, if Satan is attacking you, you are on the right path with God. Satan only leaves you alone when you belong to him. You will always go through trials because God is working in your life so you can have a better fellowship with him.

My brethren, count it all joy when ye fall into divers temptations, knowing this that the trying of your faith worketh patience - **(James l: 2-3).**

The victory is coming out of the trials and not falling victim to them.

When I was a teenager; a group of us would go downtown to the movies at midnight. It was called the owl show, because they showed scary movies starting at midnight. After the movies, we would go home in separate directions and that meant that we'd have to walk home alone.

I lived by the bayou, and I had to cross it at night. It was the most frightening thing to do. Yet I did it because I wanted to see the scary movies. That is the way it is in life. We put up with the fear when we find pleasure in what we are doing. Fear doesn't seem to stop us from sinning, because we like the sin we are committing. So why is it we are afraid of doing God's will at times? Is it because we are ashamed of the gospel?

Author's Note:

You must always be dressed in armor and

ready to do battle. You never know when the enemy will attack.

Always remember we are in constant spiritual warfare. We are in this world, but not of this world. We must be ready to do battle with our enemy because we are in his world. The primary place of attack by Satan is in the mind and thought life. It's in our thoughts, he begins his battle. You must be prepared for any surprise attacks the enemy can launch.

No weapon or tongue formed against you can prosper unless you let it.

The Bible said *to bring every thought into the captivity of Christ*.

God has a plan and so does our adversary, the devil. Remember, Satan is a great imitator. He is always trying to prove God wrong.

God's Plan	Satan's Plan
Repent	Doubt
Salvation	Discouragement
Faith	Division

Hope	Defeat
Love	Delay

Satan seeks to deceive us. His target is our mind. He will try to plant a seed in our minds (imaginations), and if we allow it to take hold, it will lead us into sin. Don't let it take hold; kill it from the start before it has a chance to become a sin. If you have the word of God in your mind, you have no room for the evil to take place. That is why it is very important to stay in the Word of God. Satan gets us to entertain fantasies, because he knows that the fantasies often turn into reality.

Imaginations are like a pregnancy, it festers in your mind and with every fantasy it begins to grow the more we feed the fantasies in our mind the more it grows until it becomes sin.

Therefore, it is imperative that we are rooted in God's truth through His Word and prayer. Our effectiveness as believers stems directly from the fact that we are made righteous through the redemptive work of Christ at Calvary, and not by our own works. We can rest assured, knowing that our steadfast trust in Jesus will enable us to carry out His work on earth. Knowing we are forgiven and cleansed by the grace of God through Christ in our daily walk with Him. Your old sin nature is gone and is replaced with a new spirit nature. We will not have the desire to sin as If Christ had never become human, an approach to his throne would be either intimidating or insolent.

Christ totally understands the human situation. He has taken part in our nature, and, therefore, understands every aspect of that nature from within. He is not hostile to humanity, but is one of us. He wants to help each of us be the kind of human being he was, and he knows how to help. When we come close to him, we approach a nature like his. Therefore, we dare to approach with boldness and confidence.

God created a wondrous world of beautiful things. Every part bears the stamp of His finger. The world, however, has another meaning. The "world" refers to the things in God's creation that pull us away from our Creator's holiness, and thus, from living in fellowship with him.

The world, in this context, is an evil system totally under the grip of Satan. This becomes concrete in wicked desire or base appetites for the things forbidden by God. Evil will eventually be conquered by Christ and removed from the world God created.

Implicitly, it has already been defeated in His death and resurrection. When he destroys it completely in his second coming, God's created world will once more have its original beauty.

In the Old Testament, Satan was understood to be a tempter who actively opposed God and his people. The New Testament presents a fuller description of Satan than did the Old Testament. This fuller understanding of Satan does not mean God must divide his sovereign power and control of history with an equally powerful demonic god. Satan holds considerable power in human history. He can even be called, "prince of this world."

Satan cannot force or tempt God to act unjustly or against God's will. As a tempter, Satan provides us with an alternative to serving God. This is part of human free will. Jesus exercised His free will to serve God and God's purposes. He showed that Satan could be defeated. He also showed that accomplishing God's purposes through Satan's method is wrong. Providing food for the hungry, displaying God's power and will to care for His own, and establishing Christ's kingdom are all part of God's ultimate purpose. Each must be done under God's leadership, not Satan's.

Suffering is temporary. As God's people, we know we will eventually receive his help and relief. Suffering is an opportunity for Satan to use our hard times to create fear, anxiety, and doubt.

The path we take as Christians are very lonely at times. It may seem at times that we have to deal with our problems without any help. We must humbly trust God and exercise self-control while we wait for his help. We gain courage by knowing we are not the only ones who must suffer. All Christians have to go through a refining process.

Why do we struggle with our Christianity? We pray, read the Bible, and do everything we can to continue on the path, yet we fall back from our Christian walk with God. I don't think that falling back is what keeps us from going again, because all we have to do is ask God for help. God will supply all the necessities needed to continue our walk. We fall back at times because of our own selfish desires.

The things that hold us back are guilty and not seeking God. We try to continue on our own, but we haven't the strength; we need the strength of Jesus. The main problem is we like the things of this world, so how do we separate ourselves from this world?

We have to draw the line and try to stay on the side of the spirit. We must isolate our self s from the things of this world that are against God, and only do the things of this world that please God. How do we tell the difference? We go back to right and wrong. Make a list of each and then do only the things that are right in God's eyes. We are selfish people, and we only want to please ourselves. Sometimes we desire something because we are spoiled. Even when God blesses us, we seek more, and that is when our pride comes into play.

Author's Note:

Has your life changed? Then act like it; a child of God walks in faith and not in pride.

The Holy Spirit is always with us to help guide us in all truths. We must never forget the indwelling work of the Holy Spirit is the promise of God and the gift of Jesus. We have the love of the bridegroom and the bride, the love which touches all human love with its inexpressible charm, and transfigures and glorifies the humblest lot and the hardest circumstances into a heavenly paradise.

Holy Spirit, whose teaching, sanctifying, and chastening are the dealings of love. He draws us unconsciously, and imperceptibly, but irresistibly away from sin and toward God. He guides us into all truth. While the Holy Spirit condemns the sin, it presents pardon to us. The Holy Spirit works in us to help us understand the GOSPEL and draw out of it that light and life which we need to grow in Christ. It's the loving Holy Spirit that baptizes seals, indwells, witnesses, helps, liberates, strengthens, teaches, and works within us. We have the Holy Spirit to turn to every time we suffer insecurity.

Not by might, nor by power, but by my Spirit, saith the Lord of hosts- **Zechariah 4: 6.**

When disaster, depression, distress, and loneliness appear, don't be tempted to give up in despair; just remember the Holy Spirit is able to break through this, and bring to mind the promise of Jesus. The Holy Spirit shines in our heart to give us the knowledge of the GLORY of GOD. The Holy Spirit enables us to receive spiritual things in a spiritual light.

Remember, we can do nothing without the Holy Spirit. For if we are filled with the Spirit, there is no room for SIN. If you take a glass and fill it up to the brim with a liquid, you cannot put any more in without it spilling. So when we are full of the Holy

Spirit, there is no room for sin to enter into our life; it will just spill out.

Our flesh: The sinful nature that lives to be gratified; unrestrained sensual appetites. Our adversary: (devil): Satan and his demonic forces tempt us to sin against God on one hand, then, when we sin, they accuse us and bring condemnation. The devil is the accuser of the brethren, and our adversary.

A soul under Satan's power and led captive by him is blind to the things of God. Satan tries to blind our eyes with unbelief, and tries to seal our lips from prayer. There is just one way of resisting the devil and that is by steadfastly believing and acting on God's word (the Bible).

Be sober, be vigilant; because your adversary the devil walks about like a roaring lion, seeking whom he may devour- **1 Peter 5:8 (NKJV)**

CHAPTER 6:
DESIRE

"Therefore, laying aside all malice, all deceit, hypocrisy, envy, and all evil speaking, as newborn babes, desire the pure milk of the word, that you may grow thereby,

1 Peter 2:1-2 (NKJV)

The desire of every Christian should be to love the Lord with all their hearts. So what's keeping us from doing just that? Is it our own selfishness? Why is it that we always want to put our own desires first instead of making God our first priority? I know that sometimes I get so carried away with simple daily tasks that sometimes I don't talk to God, as I should. But when something happens, I am the first to cry to God. Sometimes we only remember God, when we get into a bad situation. The desire of every Christian should be to have a closer walk with God.

Almost from the beginning mankind chose to disobey God. Adam and Eve considered their own desires when given a choice of what to do. They chose to disobey God. They had a pure form of worship at the beginning, they both loved God only. After they ate the fruit, they loved each other in a different way. They still loved God, but they didn't have what they had before: 100% love for God. If you take the word "*pure*" it means "*no contaminates*." There is no pure religion, because humans have tried to make religion work for them and not for God. We sin with eyes wide open because that is our nature. It's a hard battle when you have to fight your own selfish desires.

Why is it that many who do something wrong claim to be doing it in the name of God. For example, the terrorists who say they are dying for God when they are killing innocent people. What is the matter with us? Have we lost our sense of direction? Religion has been made to serve man instead of serving God. We take what is easier to follow instead of what God tells us to follow.

Why are we here on this earth? It's a question that has been asked for centuries. Have you asked yourself that question? The main reason we are here is to learn how to have fellowship with God. The angels were created to serve God, and we were created to have fellowship. The angels don't have a free will as human beings do. The only problem with a free will is that we are free to make our own decisions. That in itself sometimes gets us into trouble. Human beings take something and instead of following instructions want to change it into something different believing that it will make it easier, but that only disrupts the original way.

We are all guilty of throwing away the instructions of things that we buy and must be assembled. We think we can do it better that what the instructions say because the instructions takes too long to follow. Jesus came to do away with the old law and bring a new kind of law. The good news is that through Jesus we could be cleansed of sin. The law in itself, only showed when and how we sinned, but it did not remove sin.

Walking in the Spirit means just that—walk in the Spirit. To walk in the Spirit is to recognize the Spirit as present and abiding in us. How often, after we have asked His presence, we treat Him as if He had deceived us, and cry to Him as if He were afar off! Let us recognize Him as having come, and address Him as a present and indwelling friend.

While we are here on this earth we have to work and comply with all the earthly rules and regulations because we live here, but that doesn't mean we have to live as the worldly people do. We belong to our Lord and savior. That was our own choosing, so let's act like him and not as the people of the world. The things of the world should not matter to us. For example, we should not worry about having the best of everything. We should be comfortable with what God has provided for our daily needs.

What does humble mean? For one thing it could mean to live within our means. We learn how to have fellowship with God by putting ourselves in the right place with God. We must remember that we are the created and he is the Creator. We have to learn to live only as God would have us live.

Author's Note:

Remember faith should bring you closer to your spiritual growth and not closer to material things.

The desire of every Christian should be to worship and serve Christ. What is it, exactly, that we are looking for when we come to Christ? Are we just seeing how much we can get from Jesus? Many of us worship Jesus for the sake of certain benefits we can derive with our association with him. Some of us are looking to be healed and being blessed by Jesus because we know he provides all our needs.

Remember faith should bring you closer to your spiritual growth and not closer to material things.

We should ask how we can serve our Master more, not what can we get from him. Are we not fooling ourselves by thinking that Jesus is just merely there to serve our needs? Have we gotten so deluded with our Christianity? How can we call ourselves Christian if we find the things of God hard to follow, but the things the world has to offer easy? We do not have an open ATM from God to fill all of our needs. Are we fooling ourselves in seeing only what we want to see? As Christians, we have to look closely and discern the good from the bad. No matter how pretty the darkness is dressed to fool us, it's still dark.

We are children of the light not only based on our words but also our daily actions. We have to have the full desire of letting Jesus be Lord of our life. You may ask, "What do you mean?" Let's look at the dictionary for the definition of Lord. The Webster's Dictionary contains the following definitions:

- Ruler, governor, prince, master.
- A person having great power and authority, ruler, master.

We must let Jesus be our Master, our King, our Sovereign, and the One who has total control and authority over us. We should not do anything without his approval. Remember Jesus gave us the example "Let God's will be done," not our will.

Most of us accepted Jesus as our Lord and Savior because we wanted to get saved from our old way of life. Don't look back to what you had before you gave your life to Christ and compare it with what you have now. Do not miss the point as to why you came to Christ.

Our lives were a mess, and we needed comfort and spiritual support. We now have to keep our eyes constantly on Jesus, because the minute we look back at our old surroundings, we fall. When Moses brought the Israelites out of Egypt some of them wanted to go back to their old lifestyle. Let's see how great their life was in Egypt: they were slaves that had no control over their own destiny and had to depend on their masters. I really don't see any advantage in being in Egypt, do you? But they were willing to go back and reject God's way. Aren't we the same? We want to keep doing things our way.

As we started on our Christian walk, we were as a newborn needing nourishment to help us grow spiritually. We got the nourishment we needed from reading God's book (the Bible). We should be asking ourselves, "How can we serve God better?" as we grow spiritually.

Just because one does not feel joy, love, or peace, does not mean they are not a Christian. It only means they have to strive harder to read and study the Word. Do you not know that with every problem we go through our faith grows stronger? When we come to a problem, we don't have to handle it alone; we have our Lord Jesus Christ to lean on and he will always lift us up. Whoever said being a Christian was easy must have not been following Christ's orders. Our adversary will leave us alone if we belong to him, but when we follow Christ, he attacks.

The problem is not in starting a walk on the narrow road, but being able to finish it. Our adversary (the devil) starts to attack us the minute we start. He doesn't want us on the road to righteousness, but, rather, he wants to see us fail in our Christian walk.

- No matter what comes along, we must concentrate on continuing. It will not be an easy walk down the Path. We have to fight continuously with the world system, a system hostile to God.

- The world is always encouraging living for personal gratification, and putting our will above all else.
- The world is good at presenting a great illusion (false perception) so it can look enticing. Consequently, we do as the world does, sometimes without even thinking about it.
- The world calls out and tries to entice us into believing it has whatever we need to fulfill our lifestyle. However, it's a false promise that leads to the final destruction of our very soul.
- The world is not our friend. It tries to lure us into itself as a prostitute by showing us all it has to offer.
- The world wants to paint an illusion to make us think it can satisfy our every need.

Who is a Christian?

Anyone can say he is a Christian, but who is a Christian? That could be a hard question to answer depending on your point of view. Everybody has his own opinion as to what a Christian should be. Our mind is like our fingerprints, everybody has their own and there are no two alike. So, the real answer lies between the person and God as to whether he is a

Christian or not.

What makes you a Christian?

You must believe in your heart that you are now born-again and belong to the family of Christ. We should ask, "Where do we start, Lord?" Don't we want to be like Jesus? Those are the questions we should all ask ourselves daily.

Jesus was a very good example of what we have the potential to be. There is no mystery about it. Jesus has explained and shown us everything we need to know about being Christ-like (like Jesus Christ). We should want to be more like Christ.

Who do we want to be a slave of, self or Christ? We must make up our own mind. Ask yourself, why do I want to be a Christian? Christians must be called of God; we must be separated—dedicated—belong to God. He is beloved of God; he belongs to Christ, and he is commissioned to be a dedicated one. The will of God must be supreme. Be an ambassador for Christ, representing your master. We must always walk like Christ.

Matthew simply states that though they saw the natural meaning of the story and though they literally understood the parable, yet they did not understand its spiritual significance. **Matthew 13:10-17**

The kingdom of God is a mystery only to those who don't follow Christ. The word "mystery" in the Bible means a thing that is "concealed," or that "has been concealed." It does not mean that the thing was incomprehensible or even difficult to understand. The disciples had to know these truths. This was important for them, as they were to carry the Gospel around the world.

We, being indwelt with the Holy Spirit, should have no trouble understanding. The Bible should be read daily as spiritual nourishment for our souls as food is to our bodies. Every time a problem comes along, we don't have to face it on our own. All we have to do is turn it over to our Lord and savior.

God has given you the strength and guidance you need to resist temptations. When you became a Christian, a measure of faith was given to you. Remember that with each trial you encounter and overcome, your faith is built up to a stronger spiritual level.

The problem with most Christians is that we take for granted that God will do everything, but in reality, it is up to us to do what is morally right in God's eyes. I used to think that being a Christian was easy, but that was before I really started to serve God. I know now that a real Christian's life is very difficult at times. Especially when you are doing the Lord's work.

CHAPTER 7:
FAITH

Why do we have a hard time with our Christianity? Is it because we are supposed to live by faith and not by sight? We see the things of this world, but we cannot see the things in the kingdom of heaven. Sometimes it's hard for us to believe, because we have always been taught, "*seeing is believing,*" but the Bible teaches us just the opposite, that *the just should live by faith.* Sometimes it's hard to live by faith because we don't see the results of our prayers right away. We have to learn to trust and lean on Jesus and not our own selfish desires. Sometimes you have to trust what you can't see.

The eleventh chapter of the Epistle to the Hebrews contains the most complete treatise on faith to be found in the Scriptures. It is introduced by a definition of faith, as **"the substance of things hoped for, the evidence of things not seen.** This teaches us that faith is not hope, not a mere expectation of future things, but a present receiving of that which is promised in a real and substantial way. It is accepting and not expecting.

Author's Note:

Faith is believing without seeing. It is knowing that if you are sick and ask Christ for healing, you're healed the moment you ask.

The Bible clearly teaches that we are saved by faith or through faith. This means faith is the only instrument or channel through which we receive Christ and it is Christ, through His life, His death, and His resurrection that saves us. Faith is what brought us to Christ Jesus, and faith is what will keep us in God. Faith is believing without seeing.

Faith is knowing that if you are sick and ask Christ for healing, you're healed the moment you asked. Faith means trust in God. Through faith comes salvation. By obedience and the way we behave, we know our faith is sincere. Faith must always be motivated by love or a heartfelt appreciation of the Gospel. Faith is a Christian's heartfelt response to the love of God in his gift of Jesus Christ who was crucified for our benefit.

The first thing we must know and realize about true faith is it is our human response to the Gospel, which is always motivated by love or a deep heartfelt appreciation of Christ.

It is of utmost importance that we understand the objective facts of the Gospel, the truth as it is in Christ, without which we can never experience genuine faith.

The context of Romans 10:17 indicates that the source of faith is hearing the Gospel, the truth as it is in Christ. Jesus himself made it very clear that knowledge of him is essential.

In the parable of the sower, Christ illustrated many kinds of believers who have responded to the deceitfulness of riches choke the word, and he becomes unfruitful, but he who received seed on good ground is he who hears the word and understand it, who indeed bears fruit and produces: some a hundredfold, some sixty, some thirty.

Faith includes total submission or surrender to the objective facts of the Gospel. To live by faith alone means, above all, to live a life totally surrendered to Christ. This is what it means to walk in the Spirit. Live by faith in a prayerful attitude of absolute surrender to Christ our righteousness. Because Scripture depicts Christ's life as identifying with the indwelling Spirit of God, living by faith is the same as walking in the Spirit.

Christian living is always "not I but Christ." God will never help the flesh (self-life) to be good, for the flesh (which is Satan's domain) and God are enemies. The sinful flesh is very much alive in us and is constantly seeking to push up its ugly head.

Faith demands we maintain a humble attitude of complete submission and surrender to Christ, so that He and not our self-life may live in us, and He may manifest himself through us. It is not enough to believe about Christ; we must believe in him. The only faith that will benefit us is that which embraces him as a personal savior and which appropriates his merits to ourselves. Many hold faith as an opinion, but faith is a transaction by which those who receive Christ join themselves in covenant relationship with God. Genuine faith is life. Faith means an increase of vigor, or a confiding trust by which the soul becomes a conquering power.

Presumption: the act of presuming, an overstepping of proper bounds, or the act of taking something for granted.

Presumption is Satan's counterfeit of faith. We that have truth are secure against presumption. Faith claims God's promises and brings forth fruit in obedience. Presumption also claims promises but uses them as Satan did to excuse transgression.

Presumption is what leads to transgressing God's laws, believing that his great love would save from the consequences of sin. Faith looks beyond the difficulties and lays hold of the unseen, or even Omnipotence; therefore, it cannot be denied. Faith is the clasping of the hand of Christ in every emergency. Through faith, Christ can produce in us the very righteousness of God.

We need strong faith to see us through our darkest hour. We already know there is light at the end of the tunnel; we just have to persevere to get there. Our faith gives us the strength to persevere on our path. Let our faith hold our confidence firm until the end, remembering that the light of God's truth will shine amid the darkness that enshrouds our world. It is only with strong faith that we can withstand the trials brought upon us. God is able and willing to bestow upon us all the means to withstand any trial. It's up to us to stay on the path and walk as Christ would while trusting in God always.

We are microscopic compared to God, yet we try to dictate our needs to God. Don't you think God knows our needs before we even ask? We need to concentrate on God's plan for us and not make plans of our own and then ask God to help out with them. We seek God in times of trouble instead of seeking him because we love him for who he is.

A horse, I'm told, will stop everything and just concentrate on his pain. All his focus is on where his pain is located; nothing else matters. We as Christians should take the lesson from the horse and concentrate solely on God and bring all our focus on him; that way, we do God's will and not our own.

The things you hear from most Christians include "I need," "I want," "give me," and "everything for me, Lord." Sometimes that is all God hears from us. Where are the praises to him (prayers and worship)? Take a look at some of the other religions in the world. Some dedicate their whole lives praying to a false God. We have a living God, and we seldom pray and read the Bible, but we are quick to ask for help in times of trouble.

Why is it that Christians who have the one true God don't act like it? We need to learn to lean on Jesus rather than trust ourselves to find the correct answers to our problems. Sometimes our needs are not as big as we think, and we ask for too much. You must always remember God knows all your needs even before you do. Don't worry about wealth, health, or happiness. Learn to trust God, to turn to God, and to stay in the word of God.

When a bad thought comes into your mind, (Impure thoughts), thoughts that cause us to doubt God's love and provision for our every need or the needs of others, thoughts involving acts of sin (among these are worry, fear, envy, bitterness, discouragement, lust, pride, lying, and anger), talk to a Christian brother or sister. Tell them about the thought, and chances are the compelling thought may be eliminated. They can pray for you and give you support to overcome the thought lingering in your mind. You don't want a bad thought to stay in your mind; you must rid yourself of it by turning over to Jesus.

Some of us have been deceived into thinking sin lies in having an ungodly thought flash through our minds. We feel defeated and helpless because we do not understand that the thought itself is not sin. The important thing is what we do with the thought. If we let it remain in our mind, it may lead to sin.

We are not responsible for the thoughts coming into our mind, unless we are exposing ourselves to situations that will put the bad thought in our mind. But, we are responsible for controlling the thought, with the power of the Holy Spirit. Doubt, anxiety, anger, and nervousness can show up disrupting our physical and spiritual rest, but we are not helpless in the face of defeating thoughts.

When a bad thought comes to your mind, (thinking of an immoral action) you are induced to take pleasure in that. (This is temptation.) You like such thought and crave to retain it in your mind; you are inducing yourself into thinking more similar thoughts and seek to find pleasure in them. If you do so, you are committing sin.

Remember, we have God's armor, and temptation is just an urge toward sin. When we entertain the thought we may be in danger of yielding to it, and it is when we act on them that it becomes sin.

You can resist immoral thoughts thought Christ who gives us the strength to do away with them. Often what happens is, even when we try to erase a bad thought from our mind, it stays. Therefore we think we have sinned. It is only when we decide wholeheartedly to retain the bad thought in our mind and to think more and more on it that we really commit sin.

Therefore, even if bad thoughts linger in our minds for a long time, if we don't yield to them, we are not committing sin. If we give room for bad thoughts, and we are slightly sluggish in dismissing them, and we are not making adequate efforts to remove the thoughts. We are in danger of committing sin. Remember that when we harbor bad thoughts, it gives Satan a chance to try to make us sin. Sometimes thoughts of sin are more difficult to control than actually committing the sin itself. Trust in the Lord and the power of his might to help overcome the thought.

CHAPTER 8:
EMOTIONAL HEALING

When I was in the 4th grade, my father, who had earlier left my mother, called to say he wanted us to move with him to Detroit, Michigan. We were living in Houston, Texas, at the time. He instructed my mother to check us out of school so we could be ready to leave just as soon as he sent the train tickets. Mother did as my father asked and checked all five of us out of school. I told my friends I would be moving to Detroit and that I would not see them again.

We waited for the tickets, and they never came; my father had changed his mind about us moving there. We could not stay out of school, so we had to be checked back in. My friends thought it was a big joke. Friends can be mean at times not knowing how badly they could wound one's spirit.

It was not the first time my father had caused me emotional pain. I was hurt and disappointed, but I just put everything in the back of my mind and never dealt with it. I was full of anger and rage until the Holy Spirit showed me the cause of my hostilities. I had a hard time with my anger. Now I have an inner peace that only the Lord can give. I may struggle with my anger at times, but I know God will remove my anger completely in his timing. I have forgiven my father.

All of us have buried anger, resentment, and even rage, which began building up in early childhood. This anger often builds up over the years until it eventually reaches the boiling point. The degree of unhealed hurts, anger, and rage can be incredibly great even in those who've had a "good" childhood.

People, are affected by what is said and done to them. Over the years, if hurtful words and actions are not brought into the light of Christ, they fester like emotional cancers. Eventually they surface in problems such as anxiety, depression, addictions, compulsivity, inability for intimacy, chronic anger, eating disorders, sexual confusion, etc.

Inner healing may be needed at times to achieve the abundant, victorious life God has promised to each of us. It is the healing of emotional, mental, and physical abuse often inflicted in the early years of our lives by our parents or other family members or friends. Inner healing involves the healing of the pain of rejection, deep disappointments, and various other emotional traumas in our lives.

Inner healing is a process through which painful or traumatic memories are taken Man has three parts: body, soul, and spirit. We possess a soul (the realm of the emotions, mind and will), and we live in a body. It is within the soul realm that we find things still displeasing to God: pride, rebellion, fear, lust, unbelief, unforgiveness, rage, jealousy, emotional pain, rejection, and other areas of darkness.

The most traumatic of these hurts often come in the early years of our lives. Many of us live in denial. We try to convince ourselves we are not hurting that much, or our problem is not that serious. Many blame others and outward circumstances for the difficulties in our lives instead of having the courage to look within and recognize the need for inner healing that might change us.

The most important cause of emotional hurt comes from rejection. Rejection is the taproot to almost all of our emotional problems, particularly rejection by our mother and father.

Such rejection can come in many forms, and it can be active or passive. If we are not wanted as a child, this is passive abuse. If we are not given hugs and kisses and told we are loved, this is also passive abuse.

There can be active abuse, where we are mentally or physically abused. Mental abuse results from negative words being spoken to us like, "you are stupid," or "you are not good," and "you won't amount to much."

As little children, when we are told something of a negative nature by our parents, we believe it. It becomes established in our heart and becomes a curse in our lives, and it needs to be removed. If it is not removed, we will find that curse 87edevilling us throughout our whole life.

We may be on the edge of succeeding, and suddenly we do something that causes us to fail.

Sometimes we think we can leave the past behind, but it is still in our sub-consciousness; sooner or later we have to deal with it because if left, it may cause bitterness, anger, and it can affect the outcome of our life.

The Bible says that the Holy Spirit is the revealer of all things. We must ask the Holy Spirit to bring things to our remembrance so we can deal with them once and for all. Jesus wants you to have a sound mind.

When Satan was cast down, he had a third of the angels with him. This happened before Adam was created. What do you suppose those fallen angels have been doing all this time? They have not been lying back and enjoying life. They have been busy doing their new master's (Satan) bidding. Which involves anything that will turn you away from the truth.

They are like Satan, nothing but liars. They come into our minds and play tricks on us so we can turn away from God. Since they have been around from the beginning, they know everything about history. They can, and do, bring things from the past to make us believe we have been present in a past life.

But the Bible said we are born and then we die; nowhere in the Bible does it says once for all to die, as once for all to live. No reincarnation here. We are only reborn in the Spirit. Thanks to God and his wonderful grace.

Satan knows his time is short, and he does not want to be alone in the lake of fire. Remember:

misery loves company. Satan loves to play with your mind. That is why we must not allow our feelings to stand between God and us. If the hurts of the past are keeping us from a closer relationship with God, we need the Holy Spirit to bring inner healing of our soul.

Don't let problems rooted in the past or hurtful experiences that have not been dealt with have an effect. Have the Holy Spirit bring them out and remove them from memory. Living in the past is not Biblical; forget what lies behind.

We must not allow our emotions to stand between God and us, and if the hurts of the past are keeping us from a closer relationship with him, it is time for inner healing.

If we are determined to be changed and will cooperate with the Holy Spirit, he will bring us the deep inner healing so desperately needed. He desires to set us free, free to give love, free to receive love, and to be more than a conqueror in every area of our lives.

Inner healing may also include deliverance from evil spirits and from the curses of generational iniquity. When we come before God in prayer, he looks forward to it just as much as we do. It is a special time for him to enjoy our presence. It is his opportunity to show us his love. He delights in talking to us and in listening to us. He longs for this fellowship and misses it when we do not take time for him.

Of all the religions in the world, always remember we have the one true living God. That means we are never alone for a second, so we must live according to our calling.

especially subject to the oppression of the enemy. Only those that have grown up in Christ and understand the wily ways of this enemy can resist him effectively.

By keeping our eyes fixed on Jesus, he works miraculously in our innermost being through the Word of God and the work of the Holy Spirit, and therefore brings about what some may call "Inner Healing." God is the author of health and happiness. Satan is the author of sickness, sorrow and death.

All good is from God

Do not be deceived, my beloved brethren. Every good gift and every perfect gift is from above, and comes down from the Father of lights, with whom there is no variation or shadow of turning ***James 1:16-17(NKJV).***

All evil is from Satan.

But if you have bitter envy and self-seeking in your hearts, do not boast and lie against the truth. This wisdom does not descend from above, but is earthly, sensual, and demonic. For where envy and self-seeking exist, confusion and every evil thing are there. But the wisdom that is from above is first pure, then peaceable, gentle, willing to yield, full of mercy and good fruits, without partiality and without hypocrisy--- James 3:14-17(NKJV)

We must be prepared for this last all-out onslaught of Satan. Already this great power of darkness is increasing and great pressure is being exerted upon us. We may not even be aware of the true nature of what is responsible for our severe testing; don't look at the circumstances, just stay focused on Jesus.

Author's Note:

Most of the problems and battles we face come from the old sinful nature of self rather than evil spirits.

We as Christians have a responsibility to God. Is it so hard to completely give up all that we have in the flesh and start fresh in the spirit? Most of the problems and battles we face come from the old sinful nature of self rather than evil spirits.

The book of Job is a good example of what we go through, but in the end all things turn out well, thanks to Jesus. We must realize that many times the sickness or affliction is the result of disobedience and sin.

The most asked questions are, where is my healing Lord? And why won't some people get healed? One reason could be that when we disobey God, sickness may be permitted for God's loving discipline, because it is not God's will for us to be sick; it is God's will for us to be healed, but God has told us just how sickness may be avoided. By: Knowing what the Bible clearly teaches, Knowing that it is God's will to heal. Sufferers must be convinced by the word that their healing is the will of God. It is impossible to have real faith for healing as long as there is the slightest doubt as to its being God's will. Faith must rest on the will of God alone and not on our desires or wishes. Be sure that we are right with God, because our redemptive blessings are conditional. It is important to learn that the Lord is gracious instead of able. Most importantly be right with God before asking for healing. Some, when they see no healing, may say that the person's faith is not strong enough, but faith is not the only key ingredient? No! You have to be in the spirit and not in the flesh. Remember that you get healed because of God's promises.

Jesus died for our:

SICKNESS, PAIN, TRANSGRESSIONS,
INIQUITIES, PEACE, AND HEALING.

Jesus went to the cross in spirit, soul, and body to redeem man in spirit, soul and body. Sin is the work of the devil, so disease is also of the devil. THE HEALING OF THE BODY IS AN ESSENTIAL ELEMENT OF THE GOSPEL. Divine healing is not unconditionally promised to all Christians regardless of their conduct. Healing is for those who believe and obey; those who have faith. Until a person squarely faces and settles the question of obedience to God, he is not on believing ground. No one can successfully resist the devil until he submits himself to God. When the devil is resisted, he will not merely walk away, he will literally run. (Flee from you.) You must push Satan out of your way, and press beyond:

*SELFISHNESS	*DISOBEDIENCE
*UNCONFESSED SINS	*LUKEWARMNESS
*PUBLIC OPINION	*TRADITIONS OF MEN
*DOUBT	*DOUBLE MINDEDNESS
*SYMPTOMS FEELING	*AND THE LYING DEVIL.

Having true faith is being so convinced of the absolute truth of the declarations of God recorded in the Bible that we act on them. Faith means to receive the written promise of God as his direct message. You must praise God for your healing because to withhold praise will show either unbelief or ingratitude. There is just one way to resist the devil and that is by steadfastly believing and acting upon God's Word. So let us put sickness away by faith as we would put away sin. The consecrated Christian will not consciously tolerate sin for a moment, yet some of us are so tolerant toward sickness we will even indulge on our aches and pains instead of resisting them as the works of the devil. We think that we are suffering for Christ. Our Lord suffered and died for us already, there's no need for us to suffer. God simply steps aside sometimes and permits Satan to act against us, so we can grow stronger in our faith, so that we will be able to overcome our trails easier and gain patience at the same time. But, remember that in the case of Job, Satan could only go as far as God would permit him.

*And the Lord said to Satan, "Behold, all that he has is in your power; only do not lay a hand on his person." So Satan went out from the presence of the Lord-- **Job 1:12(NKJV)***

God permitted Satan to afflict Job to prove the faithful integrity of His servant. It also served as a refining fire to perfect his faith and make him a greater vessel of honor. As good a man as Job was, he found things to repent of when the Lord appeared to him and Job beheld his glory.

The reason our adversary is destroying us today is because of our willful ignorance of God and His Word, sinful disobedience, and unwillingness to yield to the Lord. We are no match for our adversary in our own strength; we must learn what the Scripture says, "Be strong in the Lord, and in the power of his might." (Eph. 6:10.) There will be many questions as to why we go through certain trials, but that is not our concern, we should trust Jesus to see us though and not allow the trial to defeat us. It's hard at times for us as Christians, especially when we have a death or illness in our family. Our trails sometimes may even bring us close to the brink of defeat. But we must not look at our own understanding, but God's. Remember, everything is under God's control. Under the reign of God we have his people and the myriad of angels that are ministering spirits sent forth to minister to the heirs of salvation. **(Heb. 1:14).** Some of the angels are greater in power and wisdom than others. The talents and callings of God's people vary also.

Under the reign of Satan, who is a fallen angel of a very high order, there are also a myriad of evil spirits known as demons. The world of lost, unregenerate men is likewise his instruments. Satan's kingdom is organized and divided into various provinces with fallen angels called princes over these provinces. The evil prince of Persia that withstood the archangel Gabriel to keep him from coming to Daniel is an example of such an evil prince

Then he said to me "Do not fear, Daniel, for from the first day that you set your heart to understand, and to humble yourself before your God, your words were heard; and I have come because of your words. But the prince of the kingdom of Persia withstood me twenty-one days; and behold, Michael, one of the chief princes, came to help me, for I had been left alone there with the kings of Persia-- **Daniel 10:12-13**

Satan is a lying spirit; he was so in the mouth of Ahab's prophets, and so he was in the mouth of Ananias, and by this made it appear that he filled his heart. Our God does everything in order and since Satan is a great imitator, it has been thought that the evil spirits assault us in a sort of order and method, different spirits bending all their energies to tempt us to different sins. As we read the scripture we find different kinds of evil spirits for example: a lying spirit, unclean spirit, and spirit of jealousy. Jesus said of the evil spirit, whom the disciples could not cast out. "This kind goeth not out but by prayer and fasting." Hence, it has been thought "some spirits take delight in uncleanness and defilement." Some urge us on to blasphemies, others to anger and fury. Some take delight in gloom, and others are soothed with vainglory and pride.

Each instills into our heart that vice in which he takes pleasure. Yet all do not urge their own perverseness at once, but in turn as opportunity of time or place, or as our own susceptibility invites them. Evil spirits, in their malice and rebellion, while stirring up the lust of conquest, are still God's messengers in that he overrules them; as to **Paul (2 Cor. 12:7)**, "the thorn in the flesh, the messenger of Satan to buffet him," was still the gift of God. "It was given me," he said. On occasion, God may use demons to further His purposes. He sent an evil spirit to stir up the people of Shechem against Abimelech **(Judges 9:23).** He used one to afflict Paul so that he would not become overly proud. **(2 Corinthians 12:7)**. They recognize our Lord as the Son of God. They belong to the number of those angels that "kept not their first estate, "unclean" spirits, "fallen angels," the angels of the devil. They are the "principalities and powers" against which we must "wrestle."(**Ephesians 6:12**)

CHAPTER 10:
BE PREPARED

In the era of the Cold War, there was a lot of talk about brainwashing. To brainwash someone is to indoctrinate them so intensively and thoroughly as to effect a radical transformation of their beliefs and mental attitudes.

If one country could be successful in brainwashing, then they could use the individual to spy for them. To brainwash a person takes time, and it has to be done slowly. You just don't get brainwashed overnight. That is exactly what Satan is using as one of his weapons, and that is how he is going to expose himself to us.

We will see evil and not give it a second glance because we are being brainwashed with today's media, cartoons, and movies. We see all kinds of unimaginable creatures in the movies and cartoons. We live in an age of convenience and everything is made to save time, but time seems to be slipping away.

I remember when I was younger, when time would go so slowly for me. I couldn't wait until I was

21 years old. Now, it's the other way around; time goes too quickly. Have we come to a point where we don't depend on God for our needs anymore? Have we become polluted with religion and don't really know what is right anymore?

People have different opinions about how we are to serve God. We have become too involved with modern-day life. Everything has to be, "Right now." Have we forgotten patience? The Bible says patience is a virtue. Where are we going in such a hurry? We have to slow down and smell the roses. The time of Christ's coming is closing upon us. God loves us and wants to wait until the very last minute so more of us will enter the kingdom of God. The devil, on the other hand, knows the end is near and wants to take as many as he can with him to the lake of fire. If he can deceive a third of the angels, don't you think it would be easy to fool us? He will do anything in his power to convince us that there will be no end to this world, as we know it.

Author's Note:

"Don't be caught sleeping; stay awake and be conscious that the second coming of the Lord is fast approaching. We don't know the hour or day of the corning of our Lord, and we do not need to know."

Don't be caught believing his lies. Know this: The last days are upon us. Don't be caught sleeping; stay awake and be conscious that the Second Coming of Christ is fast approaching. We don't know the hour or day of the coming of our Lord, and we do not need to know. We just need to always be on alert, just as an army at war is constantly in the state of alert.

In the story about the great flood, Noah warned the people of the coming disaster for over 125 years. The warning went unheeded. Today we are waiting for the second return of our Lord and savior, Jesus Christ. I have heard people say that they have been hearing this all of their lives, yet they see no sign of the coming of Christ. We keep on with our daily lives as if we have forever, but we don't know when Jesus will return, and we should be ready to go with him, without notice.

In Matthew 24:37-41, Jesus compares our times to the days of Noah. The world as we know it is going to end. When will it happen? Only the Father knows. We should not be worried, just be prepared. You may ask, "How can I be prepared for the end when I don't think it is ever going to happen?"

Believe me, the world will end, and we must be ready. We are sons/daughters of the living God. We have faith to see us through any situation, and we have hope of the coming of our Lord. Let's act like the children of God and not children of this world who are lost with no direction or purpose.

We have to be prepared at all times, knowing that with a twinkle of an eye we will be taken up to be with the Lord. We won't have time to say good-bye or worry about who is left behind. We won't have time to ask for forgiveness if we are in the middle of committing sin.

We have to be prepared as if the Lord is coming any second now. If we need any type of service we look in the yellow pages. You see a lot of advertisements for 24-hour service on almost anything. That means someone is just waiting for us to call so they can come out and see to our needs. We as Christians should be ready to be taken up in any given minute, not knowing the hour of Christ's return. It could be a second, minute, hour, day, week, month, year, what does it matter?

We have a responsibility to be ready. Believe that Jesus could come at any time. We need to examine our faith to see if it has been based on some form of religion or church activity and not on God. We must make sure our faith is based upon the right foundation. We must sacrifice our own personal pursuits and allow more time for prayer and studying the Word. That way, we will always be prepared to be good witnesses to our friends and neighbors and be ready for the return of our Lord.

If we read the Word for ourselves, we will know when we encounter false teachers. If we don't know the Word, we will not know if we are being taught the correct scriptures. We don't want a watered down Gospel; we want the truth and nothing but the truth. Satan always deceives though false teachers and takes us away from the simplicity of Christ.

Evil teachers began in apostolic times to creep into our churches. The Word is our only defense against the evil attacks of Satan. Perverse ones and deceivers are exposed through the truth of the Word. Don't give in to spirits that lead to error or lead to embracing corrupt and erroneous views on demonology.

- Some of the acts of demonology includes;
- **Apostasy**: The state of having rejected your religious beliefs, your political party, or a cause (often in favor of opposing beliefs or causes) renunciation, defection.
- The act of abandoning a party or cause.

- **Tergiversation:** A turning away from true Bible doctrine. Stand firm, and don't be deceived. Deception leads to anxiety and fear.

Deception in the church is commonplace, including the countless Christians who have disturbed many over the centuries with false predictions about the Lord's return. Remember Satan can disguise himself as an angel of light, and his servants also disguise themselves as servants of righteousness.

Satan cannot make us do what we do not choose. As did Jesus, we have the power to resist Satan and temptation, if our faith is strong. We can, and will be deceived by signs and wonders because we are hungry for evidence of the supernatural, so it would not be too hard for flamboyant preachers to get our attention.

They may be wrong, but with their smooth talk, they can convince people what they are saying is right. In our age of the Internet, it's relatively easy to get a minister's certificate. False prophets plague the church because they can easily deceive us with false claims and mighty works.

To recognize false prophets, the ordinary Christians must examine the lifestyles and the messages of their ministers. Does his behavior and character conform to Christ and his teaching? Does he proclaim only what people want to hear, which makes life easy and pleasurable, while ignoring the demanding and difficult requirements of discipleship? Some people would do anything for money; even con people by pretending that they are holy men of God.

CHAPTER 11: DISCERNMENT

Wouldn't it be nice if we could see things for what they really were? I mean let's say we could see into someone's inner thoughts. Would that make it easier to understand their motives? We all put on some sort of defense mechanism so we can be liked. We are afraid people will not like us the way we are. Some do it for good and others do it to take advantage of others. God has given us the gift of discernment to help us. It is sort of a weapon to protect us from being taken advantage of. We are all of a different mind, and that is why we have many different views on life, death, and God. Discernment comes from studying the Bible.

With the gift of discernment we can judge or identify the true nature of a person or a wolf among us. It is with the Holy Spirit that we receive this gift of discernment. The gift of discernment is more than identifying evil Spirits, and when coupled with the gift of wisdom becomes a powerful tool in our Spiritual Warfare. With discernment we are able to know the needs of others and with the wisdom God will show us how to help them.

Many false teachers use scriptures as a basis of their teaching. They twist and pervert the scriptures to make it fit their philosophy. As Christians we need to test what we hear and what we read by comparing it with the word of God. This is possible for a spiritual person to do. Discernment is a mark of a mature Christian. Discernment is a weapon of spiritual warfare.

Every Christian should exercise the gift of discernment, because there are many false prophets out there, and many more will come, because we are in the last days. Jesus has warned us, it's up to us to discern. To discern accurately, we must make ourselves blind to what seems so apparent.

Discernment is an important gift for our protection; it is that of, the distinguishing of spirits. The basic meaning of distinguishing has to do with separating out for examination and judging in order to determine what is genuine and what is spurious. Satan is the great deceiver, "the father of lies."

And ever since the fall, Satan and his demons have counterfeited God's message and God's work. All Christians should judge carefully what they hear and read, and "not believe every spirit, but test the spirits to see whether they are from God."

That is what the God-fearing and noble-minded Jews of Berea did when they first heard the gospel from Paul. They tested Paul's word against what they knew of God's Word, and because the two words matched, they believed what he preached was from God and not from demons.

That is what we must do with every message said to be from God, look them up in the scriptures. No preacher or teacher of the Gospel should resent having what he says judged against scripture. Some ideas given as scriptural, and on the surface seem scriptural, are actually clever counterfeits that would deceive most believers.

The gift of discernment, however, can easily deteriorate into a critical, proud, and self-righteous spirit. It can be judgmental instead of corrective when it is imitated in the flesh. But rightly used it is a great protection for us.

In the Word of God, we are repeatedly warned of deceptions and deceivers, and every minister of the Gospel should be diligent in warning the people of God to shun every false way. Jesus said, "Take heed that no man deceive you. For many shall come in my name, saying, I am Christ, and shall deceive many." Again he says, "If it were possible, they shall deceive the very elect." Paul says, "Let no man deceive you with vain words." (**Ephesians 5:6**) "Be not deceived." John says, "Little children, let no man deceive you." (**1 John 3:7**)

The New Testament abounds in such warnings, which were given for the reason that "evil men and seducers shall wax worse and worse, deceiving, and being deceived."

Let us, who value our eternal welfare, take warning and beware of deceptive spirits, false prophets, and self-delusion. The mind is the battleground for Satan. This is where we must recognize the enemy and defeat him. Through the mind He enters our being and eventually takes control of our life. This is where the fiery darts of poison are hurled. This is where the evil is conceived. Control your thoughts and Satan will be helpless.

All negative and wrong thinking eventually leads to evil. Nip it in the bud, and you will save yourself much grief and sorrow. Constant and eternal vigilance must be maintained to keep Satan from gaining a foothold.

All thoughts of evil that bring unrest and fear into your heart is from Satan. Thoughts of evil and suspicious about your fellow man, resentment provoking thoughts, thoughts that cause discouragement, gloom, and dissatisfaction with your lot in life, jealousy, hatred, lust, covetousness, and thoughts of doubt concerning the Word of God are all spawned from Satan.

We must meet every thought, temptation and trial with the word of God. The wrath of God that results from rejecting truth takes a particular form. God will turn men over to Satan and his hosts with no hope of recovery, no way to escape final judgment and Hell.

Today we are witnessing this process on a worldwide scale. Satan cannot act unless God permits it, he is a tool, an instrument of God's purpose. He has been somewhat restrained during the Church age, so that the gospel might go forth and reach the elect.

Religion is Satan's greatest tool to deceive since it is supposed to be a source of spiritual enlightenment. He has, however, used it as a spiritual trap leading to spiritual death.

The entire book of Galatians was written to counter false teachers who had hindered (5:7) and bewitched (3:1) the believers with a perversion of the

Gospel (1:7). Are we immune to this today? No, we have to be able to discern the good from the bad and we can only do that if we study God's word.

There might be some genuine believers today, with grace brought by true faith in Christ, who nonetheless are "hindered" in their efforts to serve the Lord by false doctrines.

The truth is we cannot read very far in the teachings of Jesus or any of the apostles without encountering sobering warnings concerning satanically inspired deception. Satan cannot touch the salvation of a truly born-again believer, sealed with God's Spirit, but he can sure mess up our lives if we, through ignorance or carelessness, let him.

Satan gains influence and entrance to people through lies. So why do we open up our lives to the influence and control of demons by receiving their lies? Because those lies are cleverly designed to disguise their true character and to appeal to our nature.

Demons are very skilled at helping us rationalize (justify) when we embrace falsehood. A rationale is basically a bit of reasoning to help us justify something we've already embraced in our hearts. It is a device that helps us to receive darkness and then to pacify our conscience with a fantasy that it is not really darkness after all.

That is why we are warned to cast down "imaginations" (reasoning's) "and every high thing that exalteth itself against the knowledge of God, and bringing into captivity every thought to the obedience of Christ"

The truth of God sets us free. It breaks the hold of devils and brings peace. Truth does not need a rationale to get past our conscience. It can and does walk in the light of day and simply "tells it like it is."

All of the spirits, the ones behind all of the wickedness this cursed world has ever known, are alive today; they know their time is short. Nations rise and fall. People live and die. But the spirits who inspire us to do evil don't die; they are still with us today. The simple truth is that this present world order belongs to Satan and his legions of demons. In Matt 4:1-9 during his temptation of Christ, the devil showed Him "all the kingdoms of the world in a moment of time" and then said, "All this power will 1 give thee, and the glory of them: for that is delivered unto me; and to whomsoever I will I give it." Jesus, using the word, refused the temptation but did not dispute his claim.

Evil is pure darkness. There is no trace of light in it whatsoever. There is a saying: the mind is the devils playground. Always be filled with the Spirit and allow no room for satan.

CHAPTER 12: CONCLUSION

We are the army of the Lord, and it's up to us to keep fighting the spiritual battle that has been brought upon us by our adversary when we became one with God. I have heard it said the Christian army is the only army that kills their wounded. I often wondered what it implied. I have come to the conclusion that it means that as Christians, we are quick to judge fellow Christians who have fallen short in their walk with the Lord. Instead of reaching out to them in love and compassion, we dismiss them from our social group as unworthy.

We must remember we are all in the same camp (God's camp) our adversary doesn't need our help; he does well by himself. We all have to be one in Christ. We are all members of the body, and each of us has a separate purpose. Love is what God is all about. I had a hard time with love. How can you learn to love others if you don't have any love for yourself?

Some have said that life is not fair, but isn't life what you make of it? We all went through different emotions as we were growing up. Some of us were better able to handle it than others, but nevertheless, we have things that seem to drag us down. Most of us turned to Christ for that reason. We discovered we couldn't do anything on our own but through Christ we could. We chose to serve Christ, and we did it with our own free will. We were not forced into it, so why is it so hard to stay on the path that leads to God?

I struggle with my Christianity, at times, as most do. I find myself wondering if what I'm doing is benefiting God, or if I am just going through some religious motions. God is the only honest and real person we know. Why can't we serve him to the best of our abilities? That means to surrender our whole lives to God. There is no compromise, because no one can serve two masters. Remember what Jesus said: for either we will hate one; and love the other; or else hold to one and despise the other. You cannot serve God and continue to sin. Those who do not go all the way toward God, in time, will fall by the wayside.

Who said being a Christian was easy? Sometimes the path we are on is a lonely one. I struggle, and there are a lot of people in the same boat as me. We just have to learn to lean on Jesus daily. We have been raised in an environment that demanded a great deal. As we were growing up, we were told how to eat, walk, talk, and act. When we didn't comply, we were labeled rebels because we didn't fit the mold that society had laid out for us.

A lot of us have emotional problems we tuck deep inside instead of dealing with them. God takes us as we are and will heal all our hurts, but he will heal in a slow and careful way, so that we can handle them without going into a deep depression.

God is always gentle with us until we become spiritually strong, then he can use us as mighty people of God. We have to learn to let go of our daily existence and let God direct us in the right path. I know sometimes life is not always what it is supposed to be. Many things never work out like we planned, but we are learning to turn to God for the proper purpose of our life. We are followers of Christ, and we should conduct ourselves accordingly.

We have to be an example to the world that God's way is the only Way. When we receive Christ in our life, the old nature is put away and we receive a new nature. We have to live as one with Christ. We have to live in the spirit not in the flesh by putting away our old way of thinking and learning to rely on God to direct us. We can't live the way we were, but we must live as a person of God. We are ambassadors of God and should act accordingly.

Remember the Holy Spirit is the revealer of all things and will bring to the surface what we have hidden in our innermost being. It will bring out one thing at a time so we can deal with them. We might still fall at times until all things have been brought out and that is when we should turn to Jesus. Once all things have been revealed, we will have inner peace.

Once the devil takes hold of our hand, he doesn't want to let go. He will take us to the wrong side of the road. We must let go of Satan and his world and instead grab the hand of Jesus, the one who really loves us. He died for us so we can have eternal life.

Remember, only a true friend will give his life for another. Jesus will always be waiting for us to take his hand. We don't want to be without him. Don't ever feel the relationship with Jesus is ruined when we go astray. We all make mistakes; we have to get back in fellowship with him by simply asking for forgiveness. Don't make the mistake of believing the devil when he says that we are not worthy to come back to Christ. Remember the devil is a liar. Just realize that we have sinned and ask for forgiveness.

Don't forget that a closer walk with Jesus will keeps us from sin. Let's try to stay in the Spirit and not in the flesh. When we are full of happiness and joy, we have no need to sin. Don't be lazy. As Christians instead of reading and studying the Bible, we depend on others to teach us the Word.

We need to take the time to read and study the Bible ourselves. We, as Christians, have a duty to follow Christ. How are we going to know when we are being deceived, if we don't study the Bible?

When we go on a trip we might get lost and have to ask for directions. Sometimes they are given to us incorrectly, and we have to look at the map to find our way. It is the same with the direction that God leads us. We can only find our way if we read the map (The Bible). Without the map, (The Bible), we will never get to our destination.

The question we must ask ourselves is: whom are we serving? Self – God - or Satan? The Pilgrim's Progress, a book by John Bunyan, is an allegory of a Christian's journey from the City of Destruction to the Celestial City. There was Mr. Worldly, ply able and so on. ply able was a Christian only when it was convenient. When things got too rough he didn't want to be a Christian any longer.

How many of us are doing the same thing? We have to wake up and fully realize Jesus is coming soon. All the signs are around us. If we call ourselves Christians and desire to be with our Lord, we must act like it.

Remember Jesus said that in a twinkle of an eye we would be taken up, that's not too much time. Would you have time to repent? You don't want to be left behind. That is why we should be Godly at all times.

When you make a commitment, you must fulfill it, and you made a commitment to God. We chose to serve God! So why don't we? We are always looking out for #1 (us). Let's put aside things that have no business in our life with Christ. We must direct our path with a full-hearted commitment. We wanted a better life, so we gave up the things of the world to be a follower of Christ. Why do we insist on going back to the world from time to time?

ASSORTED ENCOURAGING BIBLE VERSES

WE are not under the law, but we must be obedient to the law

That the righteous requirement of the law might be fulfilled in us who do not walk according to the flesh but according to the Spirit. -- ***Romans 8:4 (NKJV)***

For Christ is the end of the law for righteousness to everyone who believes.

By this we know that we love the children of God, when we love God and keep His commandments, for this is the love of God, and that we keep His commandments. And His commandments are not burdensome. --- ***1 John 5:2-3 (NKJV)***

Do we then make void the law through faith? Certainly not! On the contrary, we establish the law. **--- Romans 3:31 (NKJV)**

And be found in Him, not having my own

righteousness, which is from the law, but that which is through faith in Christ, the righteousness which is from God by faith.-- **Philippians 3:9 (NKJV)**

*Here is the patience of the saints; here are those who keep the commandments of God and the faith of Jesus. --- **Revelation 14:12 (NKJV)***

We are a new creation

Therefore, if anyone is in Christ, he is a new creation; old things have passed away; behold, all things have become new. -- **2 Corinthians 5:17 (NKJV)**

...By which have been given to us exceedingly great and precious promises, that through these you may be partakers of the divine nature, having escaped the corruption that is in the world through lust. -- **2 Peter 1:4 (NKJV)**

For in Christ Jesus neither circumcision nor uncircumcision avails anything, but a new creation.

Galatians 6:15 (NKJV)

Therefore we were buried with Him through baptism into death, that just as Christ was raised from the dead by the glory of the Father, even so we also should walk in newness of life. **Romans 6:4 (NKJV)**

...And that you put on the new man which was created according to God, in true righteousness and holiness. -- **Ephesians 4:24 (NKJV)**

But now we have been delivered from the law, having died to what we were held by, so that we should serve in the newness of the Spirit and not in the oldness of the letter. **Romans 7:6 (NKJV)**

Sin has no dominion over us

Likewise you also, reckon yourselves to be dead indeed to sin, but alive to God in Christ Jesus our Lord. Therefore do not let sin reign in your mortal body, that you should obey it in its lusts. And do not present your members as instruments of unrighteousness to sin, but present yourselves to God as being alive from the dead, and your members as instruments of righteousness to God. For sin shall not have dominion over you, for you are not under law but under grace what then? Shall we sin because we

are not under law, but under grace? Certainly not! --
Romans 6:11-15 (NKJV)

But put on the Lord Jesus Christ, and make no provision for the flesh, to fulfill its lusts. **Romans 13:14 (NKJV)**

If then you were raised with Christ, seek those things which are above, where Christ is, sitting at the right hand of God. Set your mind on things above, not on things on the earth. For you died, and your life is hidden with Christ in God... **Colossians 3:1-3 (NKJV)**

Who Himself bore our sins in His own body on the tree, that we, having died to sins, might live for righteousness—by whose stripes you were healed. -- **1 Peter 2:24 (NKJV)**

We have the gifts of the Holy Spirit

So we, being many, are one body in Christ, and individually members of one another. Having then gifts differing according to the grace that is given to us, let us use them: if prophecy let us prophesy in proportion to our faith. -- **Romans 12:5-6 (NKJV)**

There are diversities of gifts, but the same Spirit. -- **1 Corinthians 12:4 (NKJV**

For as the body is one and has many members, but all the members of that one body, being many, are one body, so also is Christ. -- **1 Corinthians 12: 12 (NKJV)**

But to each one of us grace was given according to the measure of Christ's gift. Therefore He says: "When He ascended on high, He led captivity captive, and gave gifts to men." (Now this, "He ascended"—what does it mean but that He also first descended into the lower parts of the earth? He who descended is also the One who ascended far above all the heavens, that He might fill all things.) And He Himself gave some to be apostles, some prophets, some evangelists, and some pastors and teachers, for the equipping of the saints for the work of ministry, for the edging of the body of Christ, till we all come to the unity of the faith and of the knowledge of the Son of God, to a perfect man, to the measure of the stature of the fullness of Christ. -- **Ephesians 4:7-13 (NKJV)**

For I say, through the grace given to me, to everyone who is among you, not to think of himself more highly than he ought to think, but to think soberly, as God has dealt to each one a measure of faith. For as we have many members in one body, but all the members do not have the same function, so we, being many, are one body in Christ, and individually members of one another. Having then gifts differing according to the grace that is given to us, let us use them: if prophecy, let us prophesy in proportion to our faith; or ministry, let us use it in our ministering; he who teaches, in teaching; he who exhorts, in exhortation; he who gives, with liberality; he who leads, with diligence; he who shows mercy, with cheerfulness. -- **Romans 12:3-8 (NKJV)**

If anyone speaks, let him speak as the oracles of God. If anyone ministers, let him do it as with the ability which God supplies, that in all things God may be glorified through Jesus Christ, to whom belong the glory and the dominion forever and ever. Amen. -- **1 Peter 4:11 (NKJV)**

Love as Christ loved

A new commandment I give to you, that you love one another; as I have loved you, that you also love one another. By this all will know that you are my disciples, if you have love for one another. -- **John**

13:34-35 (NKJV)

Since you have purified your souls in obeying the truth through the Spirit in sincere love of the brethren, love one another fervently with a pure heart. **-- 1 Peter 1:22 (NKJV)**

And above all things have fervent love for one another, for "love will cover a multitude of sins."

1 Peter 4:8 (NKJV)

My little children, let us not love in word or in tongue, but indeed and in truth. **1 John 3:18 (NKJV)**

And this is His commandment: that we should believe on the name of His Son Jesus Christ and love one another, as He gave us commandment. **-- 1 John 3:23 (NKJV)**

Beloved, let us love one another, for love is of God; and everyone who loves is born of God and knows God. **-- 1 John 4:7 (NKJV)**

No one has seen God at any time. If we love one another, God abides in us, and His love has been perfected in us. -- **1 John 4:12 (NKJV)**

Live Righteously

Flee also youthful lusts; but pursue righteousness, faith, love, peace with those who call on the Lord out of a pure heart. -- **2 Timothy 2:22 (NKJV)**

Little children, let no one deceive you. He who practices righteousness is righteous, just as He is righteous. -- *1 John 3:7 (NKJV)*

Awake to righteousness, and do not sin; for some do not have the knowledge of God. I speak this to your shame. -- **1 Corinthians 15:34 (NKJV)**

.. And be found in Him, not having my own righteousness, which is from the law, but that which i through faith in Christ, the righteousness which is from God by faith. -- **Philippians 3:9 (NKJV)**

Abide in Christ

Abide in Me, and I in you. As the branch cannot bear fruit of itself, unless it abides in the vine, neither can you, unless you abide in Me. "I am the vine, you are the branches. He who abides in me, and I in him, bears much fruit; for without me you can do nothing. If anyone does not abide in me, he is cast out as a branch and is withered; and they gather them and throw them into the fire, and they are burned if you abide in me, and my words abide in you, you will ask what you desire, and it shall be done for you. -- **John 15:4-7 (NKJV)**

He who says he abides in Him ought himself also to walk just as He walked. **1 John 2:6 (NKJV)**

And now, little children, abide in Him, that when He appears, we may have confidence and not be ashamed before Him at His coming. -- **1 John 2:28 (NKJV)**

Whoever abides in Him does not sin. Whoever sins has neither seen Him nor known Him.- **1 John 3:6 (NKJV)**

We are God's possession

Just as He chose us in Him before the foundation of the world, that we should be holy and without blame before Him in love. -- **Ephesians 1:4**

(NKJV)

Nevertheless the solid foundation of God stands, having this seal: "The Lord knows those who are His," and, "Let everyone who names the name of Christ depart from iniquity." **2 Timothy 2:19 (NKJV)**

I beseech you therefore, brethren, by the mercies of God, that you present your bodies a living sacrifice, holy, acceptable to God, which is your reasonable service. -- **Romans 12:1 (NKJV)**

Nevertheless the solid foundation of God stands, having this seal: "The Lord knows those who are His," and "Let everyone who names the name of Christ depart from iniquity." But in a great house there are not only vessels of gold and silver, but also of wood and clay, some for honor and some for dishonor. Therefore, if anyone cleanses himself from the latter, he will be a vessel for honor, sanctified and useful for the Master, prepared for every good work. **2 Timothy 2:19-21 (NKJV)**

If you were of the world, the world would love its own. Yet because you are not of the world, but I chose you out of the world, therefore the world hates you. – **John 15:19 (NKJV)**

I have given them your word; and the world has hated them because they are not of the world, just as I am not of the world, I do not pray that you should take them out of the world, but that you could keep them from the evil one. They are not of the world, just as I am not of the world. **John 17:14-16 (NKJV)**

We know that we are of God, and the whole world lies under the sway of the wicked one. **1 John 5:19 (NKJV)**

For whatever is born of God overcomes the world And this is the victory that has overcome the world our faith. Who is he who overcomes the world, but he who believes that Jesus is the Son of God? -- **1 John 5:4-5 (NKJV)**

Do not love the world or the things in the world If anyone loves the world, the love of the Father is not in him. -- **1 John 2:15 (NKJV)**

If then you were raised with Christ, seek those things, which are above, where Christ is, sitting at the right hand of God. Set your mind on things above, not on things on the earth. **Colossians 3:1-2 (NKJV)**

Pure and undefiled religion before God and

the Father is this: to visit orphans and widows in their trouble, and to keep oneself unspotted from the world. -- **James 1:27 (NKJV)**

We are no longer slaves to sin

Certainly not! How shall we who died to sin live any longer in it? Or do you not know that as many of us as were baptized into Christ Jesus were baptized into His death? Therefore we were buried with Him through baptism into death, that just as Christ was raised from the dead by the glory of the Father, even so we also should walk in newness of life. For if we have been united together in the likeness of His death, certainly we also shall be in the likeness of His resurrection, knowing this, that our old man was crucified with Him, that the body of sin might be done away with, that we should no longer be slaves of sin. For he who has died has been freed from sin. Now if we died with Christ, we believe that we shall also live with Him, knowing that Christ, having been raised from the dead, dies no more. Death no longer has dominion over Him. For the death that He died, He died to sin once for all; but the life that He lives, He lives to God. -- **Romans 6:2-10 (NKJV)**

Therefore, if you died with Christ from the basic principles of the world, why, as though living in the world, do you subject yourselves to regulations. -- **Colossians 2:20 (NKJV)**

Cleanse yourselves

Therefore, having these promises, beloved, let us cleanse ourselves from all filthiness of the flesh and spirit, perfecting holiness in the fear of God. -- **2 Corinthians 7:1 (NKJV)**

Finally, brethren, whatever things are true, whatever things are noble, whatever things are just, whatever things are pure, whatever things are lovely, whatever things are of good report, if there is any virtue and if there is anything praiseworthy—meditate on these things. **Philippians 4:8 (NKJV)**

Legally in Christ

But of Him you are in Christ Jesus, who became for us wisdom from God—and righteousness and sanctification and redemption. – **1 Corinthians 1:30 (NKJV)**

Blessed be the God and Father of our Lord Jesus Christ, who has blessed us with every spiritual blessing in the heavenly places in Christ, just as He chose us in Him before the foundation of the world, that we should be holy and without blame before Him in love, having predestined us to adoption as sons by Jesus Christ to Himself according to the good pleasure of His will, to the praise of the glory of His grace, by which He made us accepted in the Beloved. **Ephesians 1:3-6 (NKJV)**

... That in the dispensation of the fullness of the times He might gather together in one all things in Christ, both which are in heaven and which are on earth—in Him. **Ephesians 1:10 (NKJV)**

... even when we were dead in trespasses, made us alive together with Christ (by grace you have been saved), 6) and raised us up together, and made us sit together in the heavenly places in Christ Jesus... **-- Ephesians 2:5-6 (NKJV)**

But now in Christ Jesus you who once were far off have been brought near by the blood of Christ. **-- Ephesians 2:13 (NKJV)**

Alive to God

Most assuredly, I say to you, he who hears my word and believes in Him who sent me has everlasting life, and shall not come into judgment, but has passed from death into life. **John 5:24 (NKJV)**

But these are written that you may believe that Jesus is the Christ, the Son of God, and that believing you may have life in His name. Romans 6:11 (NKJV) Likewise you also, reckon yourselves to be dead indeed to sin, but alive to God in Christ Jesus our Lord. **John 20:31 (NKJV)**

And if Christ is in you, the body is dead because of sin, but the Spirit is life because of righteousness. -- **Romans 8:10 (NKJV)**

Whoever believes that Jesus is the Christ is born of God, and everyone who loves Him who begot also loves him who is begotten of Him. -- **1 John 5:1 (NKJV)**

We are the Light for the world

You are the light of the world. A city that is set

on a hill cannot be hidden. **Matthew 5:14 (NKJV)**

You are all sons of light and sons of the day. We are not of the night, nor of darkness. **1 Thessalonians 5:5 (NKJV)**

Nor do they light a lamp and put it under a basket, but on a lamp stand, and it gives light to all who are in the house. 16) Let your light so shine before men, that they may see your good works and glorify your Father in heaven. -- **Matthew 5:15-16 (NKJV)**

For you were once darkness, but now you are light in the Lord Walk as children of light... **Ephesians 5:8 (NKJV)**

Walk as God's children

Therefore be imitators of God as dear children. -- **Ephesians 5:1 (NKJV)**

For you were once darkness, but now you are light in the Lord Walk as children of light... **Ephesians 5:8 (NKJV)**

Therefore gird up the loins of your mind, be sober, and rest your hope fully upon the grace that is to be brought to you at the revelation of Jesus Christ; as obedient children, not conforming yourselves to the former lusts, as in your ignorance... -- **1 Peter 1:13-14 (NKJV)**

We have Christ's love

Now hope does not disappoint, because the love of God has been poured out in our hearts by the Holy Spirit who was given to us.-- **Romans 5:5 (NKJV)**

But earnestly desire the best gifts. And yet I show you a more excellent way. **1 Corinthians 12:31 (NKJV)**

Though I speak with the tongues of men and of angels, but have not love, I have become sounding brass or a clanging cymbal. And though I have the gift of prophecy, and understand all mysteries and all knowledge, and though I have all faith, so that I could remove mountains, but have not love, I am nothing. And though I bestow all my goods to feed the poor, and though I give my body to be burned, but have not love, it profits me nothing. Love suffers long and is kind; love does not envy; love does not parade itself, is not puffed up; does not behave rudely, does not seek its own, is not provoked, thinks no evil; does not rejoice in iniquity, but rejoices in the truth; bears all things, believes all things, hopes all things, endures all things. Love never fails. But whether there are prophecies, they will fail; whether there are tongues, they will cease; whether there is knowledge, it will vanish away. For we know in part and we prophesy in part. But when that which is perfect has come, then that which is in part will be done away. When I was a child, I spoke as a child, I understood as a child, I thought as a child; but when I became a man, I put away childish things. For now we see in a mirror, dimly, but then face to face. Now I know in part, but then I shall know just as I also am known. And now abide faith, hope, love, these three; but the greatest of these is love. -- **1 Corinthians 13:1-13 (NKJV)**

But whoever keeps His word; truly the love of God is perfected in him. By this we know that we are in Him. -- **1 John 2:5 (NKJV)**

Whoever believes that Jesus is the Christ is born of God, and everyone who loves Him who begot also loves him who is begotten of Him. -- **1 John 5:1 (NKJV)**

We live in this world, but are not of this world

... Who gave Himself for our sins, that He might deliver us from this present evil age, according to the will of our God and Father... -- **Galatians 1:4 (NKJV)**

But God forbid that I should boast except in the cross of our Lord Jesus Christ, by whom the world has been crucified to me, and I to the world. For in Christ Jesus neither circumcision nor uncircumcision avails anything, but a new creation.

And do not be conformed to this world, but be transformed by the renewing of your mind, that you may prove what is that good and acceptable and perfect will of God. **Romans 12:2 (NKJV)**

Do not love the world or the things in the world. If anyone loves the world, the love of the Father is not in him. For all that is in the world—the lust of the flesh, the lust of the eyes, and the pride of life is not of the Father but is of the world. And the world is passing away, and the lust of it; but he who does the will of God abides forever. -- **1 John 2:15-17 (NKJV)**

Pure and undefiled religion before God and the Father is this: to visit orphans and widows in their trouble, and to keep oneself unspotted from the world. -- **James 1:27 (NKJV)**

Adulterers and adulteresses! Do you not know that friendship with the world is enmity with God? Whoever therefore wants to be a friend of the world makes himself an enemy of God. **James 4:4 (NKJV)**

We are slaves of God

For he who is called in the Lord while a slave is the Lord's freedman. Likewise he who is called while free, is Christ's slave. You were bought at a price; do not become slaves of men. **1 Corinthians 7:22-23 (NKJV)**

But now having been set free from sin, and having become slaves of God, you have your fruit to holiness, and the end, everlasting life. -- **Romans 6:22 (NKJV)**

But God be thanked that though you were slaves of sin, yet you obeyed from the heart that form of doctrine to which you were delivered and having been set free from sin, you became slaves of righteousness. I speak in human terms because of the weakness of your flesh. For just as you presented your members as slaves of uncleanness, and of lawlessness leading to more lawlessness, so now present your members as slaves of righteousness for holiness. **Romans 6:17-19 (NKJV)**

... Not lagging in diligence, fervent in spirit, serving the Lord... -- **Romans 12:11 (NKJV)**

Therefore, since we are receiving a kingdom, which cannot be shaken, let us have grace, by which we may serve God acceptably with reverence and godly fear. –

Hebrews 12:28 (NKJV)

We are made holy

... Just as He chose us in Him before the foundation of the world, that we should be holy and without blame before Him in love... **Ephesians 1:4 (NKJV)**

If anyone defiles the temple of God, God will destroy him. For the temple of God is holy, which temple you are. -- **1 Corinthians 3:17 (NKJV)**

Therefore, holy brethren, partakers of the heavenly calling, consider the Apostle and High Priest of our confession, Christ Jesus... -- **Hebrews 3:1 (NKJV)**

Little children, let no one deceive you. He who practices righteousness is righteous, just as He is righteous. -- **1 John 3:7 (NKJV)**

But as He who called you is holy, you also be holy in all your conduct, because it is written, "Be holy, for I am holy." -- **1 Peter 1:15-16 (NKJV)**

Therefore, beloved, looking forward to these things, be diligent to be found by Him in peace, without spot and blameless... **2 Peter 3:14 (NKJV)**

We are free from sin's slavery

And you shall know the truth, and the truth shall make you free." They answered Him, "We are Abraham's descendants, and have never been in bondage to anyone. How can you say, 'You will be made free?" Jesus answered them, "Most assuredly, I say to you, whoever commits sin is a slave of sin. And a slave does not abide in the house forever, but a son abides forever. Therefore if the Son makes you free, you shall be free indeed. -- **John 8:32-36 (NKJV)**

Now if we died with Christ, we believe that we shall also live with Him. – **Romans 6:8 (NKJV)**

For the law of the Spirit of life in Christ Jesus has made me free from the law of sin and death. **Romans 8:2 (NKJV)**

But now having been set free from sin, and having become slaves of God, you have your fruit to holiness, and the end, everlasting life. – **Romans 6:22 (NKJV)**

Stand fast therefore in the liberty by which Christ has made us free, and do not be entangled again with a yoke of bondage. – **Galatians 5:1 (NKJV)**

For you, brethren, have been called to liberty; only do not use liberty as an opportunity for the flesh, but through love serve one another. For all the law is fulfilled in one word, even in this: "You shall love your neighbor as yourself." – **Galatians 5:13-14**

(NKJV)

Now the Lord is the Spirit; and where the Spirit of the Lord is, there is liberty. But we all, with unveiled face, beholding as in a mirror the glory of the Lord, are being transformed into the same image from glory to glory, just as by the Spirit of the Lord. **2 Corinthians 3:17-18 (NKJV)**

Live unto God

For if we live, we live to the Lord; and if we die, we die to the Lord Therefore, whether we live or die, we are the Lord's. – **Romans 14:8 (NKJV)**

And He died for all, that those who live should live no longer for themselves, but for Him who died for them and rose again. – **2 Corinthians 5:15 (NKJV)**

For I through the law died to the law, that I might live to God. 20) I have been crucified with Christ; it is no longer I who live, but Christ lives in me; and the life, which I now live in the flesh I live by faith in the Son of God, who loved me and gave Himself for me. **Galatians 2:19-20 (NKJV)**

Teaching us that, denying ungodliness and worldly lusts, we should live soberly, righteously, and godly in the present age... -- **Titus 2:12 (NKJV)**

Legal righteousness

For in it the righteousness of God is revealed from faith to faith; as it is written, "The just shall live by faith." – **Romans 1:17 (NKJV)**

But now the righteousness of God apart from the law is revealed, being witnessed by the Law and the Prophets... – **Romans 3:21 (NKJV)**

Even the righteousness of God, through faith in Jesus Christ, to all and on all who believe. For there is no difference; for all have sinned and fall short of the glory of God, being justified freely by His grace through the redemption that is in Christ Jesus, whom God set forth as a propitiation by His blood, through faith, to demonstrate His righteousness, because in His forbearance God had passed over the sins that were previously committed, to demonstrate at the present time His righteousness, that He might be just and the justifier of the one who has faith in Jesus. -- **Romans 3:22-26 (NKJV)**

What then shall we say that Abraham our father has found according to the flesh? For if Abraham was justified by works, he has something to boast about, but not before God. For what does the Scripture say? "Abraham believed God, and it was accounted to him for righteousness." Now to him who works, the wages are not counted as grace but as debt. But to him who does not work but believes on Him who justifies the ungodly, his faith is accounted for righteousness, 6) just as David also describes the blessedness of the man to whom God imputes righteousness apart from works... – **Romans 4:1-6 (NKJV)**

For if by the one man's offense death reigned through the one, much more those who receive abundance of grace and of the gift of righteousness will reign in life through the One, Jesus Christ. – **Romans 5:17 (NKJV)**

But of Him you are in Christ Jesus, who became for us wisdom from God—and righteousness and sanctification and redemption... – **1 Corinthians 1:30 (NKJV)**

And be found in Him, not having my own righteousness, which is from the law, but that which is through faith in Christ, the righteousness which is from God by faith. – **Philippians 3:9 (NKJV)**

Cleansed

You are already clean because of the word, which I have spoken to you. – **John 15:3 (NKJV)**

But if we walk in the light as He is in the light, we have fellowship with one another, and the blood of Jesus Christ His Son cleanses us from all sin. If we say that we have no sin, we deceive ourselves, and the truth is not in us. If we confess our sins, He is faithful and just to forgive us our sins and to cleanse us from all unrighteousness. -- **1 John 1:7-9 (NKJV)**

We are no longer slaves to sin

Certainly not! How shall we who died to sin live any longer in it? Or do you not know that as many of us as were baptized into Christ Jesus were baptized into His death? Therefore we were buried with Him through baptism into death, that just as Christ was raised from the dead by the glory of the Father, even so we also should walk in newness of life. For if we have been united together in the likeness of His death, certainly we also shall be in the likeness of His resurrection, knowing this, that our old man was crucified with Him, that the body of sin might be done away with, that we should no longer be slaves of sin. For he who has died has been freed from sin. Now if we died with Christ, we believe that we shall also live with Him, knowing that Christ, having been raised from the dead, dies no more. Death no longer has dominion over Him. For the death that He died, He died to sin once for all; but the life that He lives, He lives to God. – **Romans 6:2-10 (NKJV)**

Therefore, if you died with Christ from the basic principles of the world, why, as though living in the world, do you subject yourselves to regulations. – **Colossians 2:20 (NKJV)**

Indwelt with the Holy Spirit

Do you not know that you are the temple of God and that the Spirit of God dwells in you? **1 Corinthians 3:16 (NKJV)**

Or do you not know that your body is the temple of the Holy Spirit who is in you, whom you have from God, and you are not your own? For you were bought at a price; therefore glorify God in your body and in your spirit, which are God's. – **1 Corinthians 6:19-20 (NKJV)**

And what agreement has the temple of God with idols? For you are the temple of the living God. As God has said: "I will dwell in them and walk among them. I will be their God, and they shall be my people." – **2 Corinthians 6:16 (NKJV)**

But you are not in the flesh, but in the Spirit, if indeed the Spirit of God dwells in you. Now if anyone does not have the Spirit of Christ, he is not His. And if Christ is in you, the body is dead because of sin, but the Spirit is life because of righteousness. – **Romans 8:9-10 (NKJV)**

I say then: Walk in the Spirit, and you shall not fulfill the lust of the flesh. For the flesh lusts against the Spirit, and the Spirit against the flesh; and these are contrary to one another, so that you do not do the things that you wish. – **Galatians 5:16-17 (NKJV)**

If we live in the Spirit, let us also walk in the Spirit. – **Galatians 5:25 (NKJV)**

And do not grieve the Holy Spirit of God, by whom you were sealed for the day of redemption. **Ephesians 4:30 (NKJV)**

And do not be drunk with wine, in which is dissipation; but be filled with the Spirit... **Ephesians 5:18 (NKJV)**

Do not quench the Spirit. – **1 Thessalonians 5:19 (NKJV)**

Blessed assurance

... Who are kept by the power of God through faith for salvation ready to be revealed in the last time. – **1 Peter 1:5 (NKJV)**

There is therefore now no condemnation to those who are in Christ Jesus, who do not walk according to the flesh, but according to the Spirit. – **Romans 8:1 (NKJV)**

My sheep hear my voice, and I know them, and they follow Me. And I give them eternal life, and they shall never perish; neither shall anyone snatch them out of my hand. **John 10:27-28 (NKJV)**

Therefore, brethren, be even more diligent to make your call and election sure, for if you do these things you will never stumble... – **2 Peter 1:10 (NKJV)**

Therefore, brethren, having boldness to enter the Holiest by the blood of Jesus, by a new and living way which He consecrated for us, through the veil, that is, His flesh, and having a High Priest over the house of God, let us draw near with a true heart in full assurance of faith, having our hearts sprinkled from an evil conscience and our bodies washed with pure water. **Hebrews 10:19-22 (NKJV)**

For our gospel did not come to you in word only, but also in power, and in the Holy Spirit and in much assurance, as you know what kind of men we were among you for your sake. **1 Thessalonians 1:5 (NKJV)**

Adopted children of God

... Having predestined us to adoption as sons by Jesus Christ to Himself, according to the good pleasure of His will... – **Ephesians 1:5 (NKJV)**

For you are all sons of God through faith in Christ Jesus .—**Galatians 3:26 (NKJV)**

Behold what manner of love the Father has bestowed on us, that we should be called children of God! Therefore the world does not know us, because it did not know Him. **1 John 3:1 (NKJV)**

The Spirit Himself bears witness with our spirit that we are children of God... **Romans 8:16 (NKJV)**

Empowered for witnessing

Behold, I send the Promise of My Father upon you; but tarry in the city of Jerusalem until you are endued with power from on high. – **Luke 24:49 (NKJV)**

But you shall receive power when the Holy Spirit has come upon you; and you shall be witnesses to Me in Jerusalem, and in all Judea and Samaria, and to the end of the earth. **Acts 1:8 (NKJV)**

But we have this treasure in earthen vessel that the excellence of the power may be of God and not of us. **2 Corinthians 4:7 (NKJV)**

Now to Him who is able to do exceedingly abundantly above all that we ask or think, according to the power that works in us... – **Ephesians 3:20 (NKJV)**

For God has not given us a spirit of fear, but of power and of love and of a sound mind. **2 Timothy 1:7 (NKJV)**

*And my speech and my preaching were not with persuasive words of human wisdom, but in demonstration of the Spirit and of power...—***1 Corinthians 2:4 (NKJV)**

Finally, my brethren, be strong in the Lord and in the power of His might. That I may know Him and the power of His resurrection, and the fellowship of His sufferings, being conformed to His death... – **Ephesians 6:10 (NKJV)**

I can do all things through Christ who strengthens me. – **Philippians 4:13 (NKJV)**

MORE BOOKS BY HENRY MIRANDA

ETERNAL LIFE is an excellent description of the path described by Jesus Christ. Henry's insights are backed by specific reference to scripture and provide clear answers to questions that many of us have. The text is an easy ready to understand and proceeds in a logical manner to provide insight on how to walk the narrow path. The text gives comfort to those who are in need of God's presence by giving clear descriptions of how the doors to the Kingdom of Heaven are always open and how we can enter by accepting Jesus Christ as our Savior. The text describes the presence of the Holy Spirit and aids in understanding our relationship with God

YOU'VE BEEN WARNED is a biblical account of scripture with layman understanding. Henry shares his point of view, what various scriptures mean. This is a good read for those struggling with their faith, or have doubt the

existence of God. Anyone can understand this book. The Bible warns us of the deceptions of Satan. He can transform himself into an Angel of light. That could be deceiving, if we weren't in the word of God. Only spiritual maturity and insight can protect us from Satan, the master of deceit

THE PATH TO ETERNAL LIFE gives comfort to those who are in need of God's presence by giving clear descriptions of how the doors to the Kingdom of Heaven are always open and how we can enter by accepting Jesus Christ as our Savior. The text explains the presence of the Holy Spirit, and aids in understanding our relationship with God and Jesus Christ. This book is a must read for the seeker and new Christian! It's also a good reminder for the mature Christian that we should never take our Salvation for granted. Soundly based on the Word of God, each chapter topics are supported with verses of relevant Scripture. The Path to Eternal Life is not deep in philosophy, religion, or difficult doctrine, it's simply from the heart of a man who knows the true meaning of once lost and now walking the path of righteousness' based on the Bible. The Path of Life is a well-written book that will be a great blessing to all who seek this path to its fullest. Henry shares his testimony that plants a seed, nurtures and reaps. It is important that we all share our individual testimonies to help guide the lost to the path to eternal life. This book closes with precious testimonies of a few who have made the choice to live for Christ and discovered their true purpose in life.

<u>BEWARE THE WINDS OF DOCTRINE</u> is the study of the Word of God. This book explains that it's not IF we believe---it's WHAT we believe. Religion is a tool of Satan and he has placed many false teachers and preachers in our midst. This is one way that he can get to people as they have the need to worship. As the winds blow here and there so do many preachers who turn away from the Word of God to become people-pleasers. They lead their congregations down the wrong road. As a Christian we should study the Word of God diligently and know for our self if what we are hearing from the pulpit or the televised evangelists is correct doctrine or are we being deceived. The author backs his text with plenty of scripture references. We need to study to make sure what we are hearing is in accordance with scripture. .This book has pertinent information and should be read along with the scriptures.

ABOUT THE AUTHOR

Henry Miranda is an Author, Bible teacher, writer and evangelist, Henry Miranda, is the author of five life-changing books. Holding a Bachelor of Christian Ministry degree @ <u>Christian Leadership University</u>. http://www.evangelize-for-jesus-ministries.com/

God anointed me with the gift of an evangelist with the ministries of healing and deliverance. I completed four years of Bible College and earned a Bachelor of Christian Ministry degree @ Christian Leadership University If you recall the first part of the story of Jonah, Jonah tried to run away from his responsibilities, but eventually God had Jonah complete the tasks that he had set before him. So too, I chose not to get too involved in the ministry the Lord had for me and basically I didn't pursue His will as I should have.

In 1990 I was prompted by the Holy Spirit to write Christian books. God directed me to write books. By writing these books I try to bring people into God's kingdom. With the help of the Holy Spirit I have written five Christian books. I believe it is my calling to bring others closer to God through the world of publishing. Henry Miranda is an Evangelist,

Bible teacher, author and has written five Christian books.

Made in the USA
Columbia, SC
29 October 2024